Let's Speak
Arabic

Learn Arabic Conversation in just one week!

S.A. Rahman

Professor of Arabic
Centre of Arabic and African Studies
Jawaharlal Nehru University, New Delhi

Goodword Books

First published 2002
Reprinted 2003, 2005
© Goodword Books 2005

Goodword Books Pvt. Ltd.
1, Nizamuddin West Market
New Delhi- 110 013
e-mail: info@goodwordbooks.com
Printed in India

www.goodwordbooks.com

Contents

3

Introduction

This book has been prepared to serve dual purpose to help the regular students of Arabic courses to be able to speak Arabic through specially designed courses basing their eyes on the Arabic script and to enable the self-learners for specific and temporal purpose of visiting an Arabic speaking area for short or long periods of work. For this category of self-learners we have used Roman script with specially designed equivalents or let us say near equivalents for some very typical only Arabic sounds. Therefore, it becomes very necessary here to talk about and explain Arabic sounds which, when written, are called letters.

As we have known, Arabic alphabet consists of twenty-eight letters. All of these twenty eight letters are consonant letters, however, three of them function as 'elongative vowels'. These three letters are alif ا, waw و and ya ى. How and where these are used as elongative vowels, shall be explained at appropriate place.

We said, generally accepted there are twenty-eight consonant letters in the Arabic alphabet. However, for our convenience we can consider them to be thirty letters including ta marboota i.e. round ta ة and the hamza ء which are otherwise passed on as another form of normal stretched ta ت and alif ا respectively. In fact, there is no harm in considering them as 29th and 30th letters. More so because they play crucial and independent role in the formation of Arabic words- ta marboota is always used as terminal letter indicating that the nouns ending thus are generally feminine gender nouns while hamza is severally used only as consonant as against alif which is used as elongative vowel also.

In our lessons we have terminated the nouns ending in the round ta with an 'a' only, e.g. طـــالبـة meaning 'a girl student' has been written as ṭā li ba and غـرفة meaning 'a room' has been written as ghor fa and so on.

In this book in lesson one itself we have very clearly specified Roman substitutes for Arabic sounds and hence, those who would like to learn to speak through the Roman script, they should learn Roman symbols very well with emphasis on correct pronunciation.

Each language of the world would have certain things that would be very peculiar of that language and that language when spoken would sound good and give the right meanings when pronounced correctly. Keeping this in mind, let us mention here some tips to say the Arabic sounds correctly or near-correctly.

The first and the second letters of the Arabic alphabet are simple and easy to say. The third letter is soft 't' as generally spoken by the Arabs and other groups of foreigners to the English language. The fourth letter is said as 'th' in 'the' or 'Elizabeth' etc. Fifth letter is said like 'J'. The sixth letter is deep glottal aspirate 'H' which is hard to find an equivalent. The seventh letter is said as 'ch' together in 'Munich' or 'loch'. This sound can be best compared with snoring sound. Eighth letter is soft 'd' while the ninth letter is said as 'dh' together as in 'dhow'. Tenth letter is ordinary 'r' while the eleventh letter sounds like 'z' as in zebra. The twelfth letter is said like 's' and thirteenth letter is pronounced like 'sh' as in 'shank'. Fourteenth letter is said like 'ss' as in 'blessed' while the fifteenth letter is pronounced like 'd' as in 'bad'. Sixteenth letter is said like 't' in 'bat' while the seventeenth sound is not easy to give equivalent of. This can best be compared with 'echoed z'. Eighteenth letter is deep glottal 'a'. Nineteenth sound is said exactly like Parisian 'r'. This sound can be compared with 'strong gurgle' sound. Twentieth letter is comparable with 'f' and the twenty -first sound is glottal 'k', which is often replaced by the English letter 'q' as in Quran. The next sound that is the twenty second letter is said like 'n'. Twenty seventh and twenty eighth letters are said like 'w' and 'y' respectively. Then we have the round ta(ة)and hamza ء we have mentioned in the foregoing. We have given Roman equivalents in lesson one which have to be taken note of and learnt by heart if you were to learn speaking through the Roman script.

We have said that all the twenty-eight (or say thirty) letters are consonant letters and alif ا, waw و and ya ى are also used as elongative vowels. This statement might create the feeling that there are no vowels in the Arabic language. The Arabic language does have vowels as explained below. We also provide here information and symbols as we have used them in this book to say our words. VOWELS

1. First Arabic vowel is a diagonal mark above a letter written thus: e.g.أ and بَ etc.

Only in case of alif which is generally used as letter number one in al الـ we have decided to show as 'a', however in all other letters we have decided to show it as 'a' preceded by the relevant sound. e.g. بَ will be written as 'ba', تَ will be written as ta and so on so forth. In Arabic grammar terminology this is called fatHa.

2. Second Arabic vowel is again a digonal mark below a letter

7

written thus e.g. ‍ا andب

In our lessons we have shown ا as i while ب etc. have been shown as 'bi','ti' etc.

This symbol or mark is called Kasrah.

3. The third Arabic vowel is a stomached comma always written above a letter thus ‍ءe.g.اُ and بُ. In our lessons we have shown اُ as ö and بُ as bö.

This vowel mark is called *d*amma in Arabic.

Note: Hamza bearing vowel marks has been written as 'aa/ 'ai/ 'aã etc.

We have to mention here that these vowel marks may have to be necessarily written in 'twos' always below or above the terminal letters of the largest majority of nouns. In this case they are called double fat*H*a, double kasra and double *d*amma. These have been indicated in our lessons as: ön e.g. in ki tã bön, an: e.g. ban in Ki tã ban, in e.g. bin in ki tã bin etc.

These terminal vowels determine the case of a noun in terms of nominative, accusative and genitive cases. As we earlier spoke that alif, waw and ya beside being consonant letters, function also as elongative vowels provided that each one of them is preceded by a single even vowel mark, e.g. when alif is preceded by single fat*H*a likeلــ‍ـبَ, in this case it would be read and said as bã and we have shown such combinations as bã and tã etc. Where waw is preceded by *d*amma, we have decided to show them as bo and to etc in our lessons. When ya is preceded by kasra, we have written them as bi and ti etc. A single vowelled letter in itself is a syllable, like ka ta

8

ba كَتَبَ consisting of three letters ka كَ ta تَ ba بَ is a 3-syllabled word. It would obtain also with two letters together in words wherein a vowel letter is followed by a silenced letter. For example in case of مَكْتَبُ mak ta bön ma and silenced ka toghether make a syllable while following ta with fatHa makes the second syllable of the word and ba with fatHa makes the third syllable and hence this word with four letters comprises three syllables. This silencing vowel is called sökŏn and it is represented by a small circle 'o' or a right to left half circle . It is always written above a letter. When this vowel symbol is placed above the terminal letter of a word, then the word is said to be in the apocopate form. There may be words which could consist of one letter, however, it is said twice, e.g. حُبُّ Hob bon (love). In this case the letter is written single and a 3-toothed symbol ˜ is placed above that letter. Vowel marks *d*amma and fatHa are written above this symbol, e.g. ´˜ and ˜ while kasra may be written below this symbol ˷ or below the letter ˷. This symbol is called Šadda. When waw and ya are preceded by fatHa then this combination makes diphthong, e.g. bay na بَيْنَ (between). We have chosen to write this combination of fatHah followed by ya as 'ay' as in bay na. The combination of fatHa followed by waw as in "qawl" has been represented by 'aw' as in قَـوْل qawl (word/utterance).

Though in written Arabic we have to be very grammatical, however, spoken Arabic is quite different. We drop and ignore many grammatical points in spoken Arabic. In our lessons in hand, we have also dropped and ignored many things. We have concentrated to make it more workable to learn to speak rather than learn to read and write. So, this book is good for those who have no previous knowledge of written standard Arabic and who don't aim at that. If they work to acquire the Roman script as we have determined and used in this book, we are sure they will achieve good results. For those who have previous knowledge of written standard Arabic, they will relish and enjoy this book as they would realize that by following a guided path they can fruitfully use the language they already knew, and it is for them very specifically that we have used Arabic script also. Though not much grammar has been loudly used in these lessons, however, no lesson is devoid of grammar and in this way we have enhanced the utility of this book for them. Since this book has been basically prepared to learn speaking of Arabic, therefore, any detailed explanation on Arabic grammar would be a deviation from the target because no language can ever be spoken with grammar in mind. We should rather concentrate on pattern sentences.

We have given a lot of general vocabulary to enrich the stock of the learner upon which he can draw for conversation. Generally, plurals of nouns have been given. We don't intend to discuss here varieties of plural as this would not benefit much those who use the Roman script and those who know Arabic would surely be knowing this. All Arabic nouns may be considered as masculine unless they specifically mean feminine objects. Nouns terminating with the round ta ة are generally feminine. Plurals of non-personal nouns i.e. objects other than humanbeings are treated as singular of feminine gender. Common nouns generally terminate with nunnation i.e. double fatHa, double kasra and double damma. They are defined with the definite article al ال which allows only single vowel point at the terminal letter.

However, in spoken Arabic terminal letters are generally silenced and so we have generally shown them in the Roman script,however, in the Arabic part of it we have generally mentioned the vowel mark of the terminal letters of the words. Since Arabic alphabet is divided in two groups- sun letters and moon letters, therefore, when we prefix 'al' to a noun, it proves its function and utility. When 'al' is prefixed to a noun which begins with a sun letter then alif of 'al' is straightaway joined to the sun letter leaving la i.e. ل of ال unpronounced. For example ra jö lön رجـل (a man) begins with ra ر which is a sun letter, therefore, we would read/say it with the definite article al ال prefixed to it as 'ar ra jö lö' اَلـرَّجُـلُ (the man). However, in the case of nouns which begins with moon letters 'al' is full mouthedly pronounced, e.g. ki tä bön كِتـابٌ. When 'al' ال is prefixed to it, it would read as 'al ki tä bö' اَلْكِتَابُ.

It may be noted that syllables of a word are spaced as far as possible to enable the learners through the Roman script to say words with correct break-up and accent. For example كِتـــاب is written as ki tä bön and محمد as mö Ham mad etc.

Care has also been taken that a single word in Romans should be written together without splitting it in two lines. However, our success is not hundred percent. At places we have been compelled to split the word for want of space in the line. We have written our lessons in three columns. One column each for Arabic, Roman transcription and the English meaning of the Arabic text in a matching way so that the one who handles this book would not find much difficulty in comprehending the exact intended meaning of the Arabic text. However, given the different families of the

11

of the Arabic text. However, given the different families of the two languages and the character of the written shapes of the words and the placement of verbs, nouns and other supportive particles, at places we have failed to maintain our cherished style. However, our success rate is more than ninety percent.

Arabic numerals are considered nouns (though adjectival). As shown in lesson no. 15, we always use in written Arabic, numerals terminating with the round ة to qualify the masculine gender nouns and the numerals without the round ta ة to qualify the feminine gender nouns. However, not much attention is paid to this grammatical point like in case of other grammatical points. We must know that our progress in any spoken language shall be tardy if we care to be conscious about grammar and use only grammatically correct language in all aspects. This is more true of Arabic which is considered to be distant from its written standard form. Our book in hand has been specially made for people to practice speaking Arabic and that is precisely the reason that at places it would appear to be deviating from the right kind of Arabic as is insisted on by the Indian Scholars of the Arabic language. In our book at places the last letter of a word is silenced for no obvious grammatical reason. At places definite article has been loudly said despite the fact that it bedecks a noun which begins with a sun letter and so on so forth - quite un-matching the grammatical provisions.

Let me caution here the users of this book that at the early stage of learning they should seek the learned help to acquire the correct pronunciation of Arabic words and the style of delivery of Arabic sounds. We must understand that we learn faster any language in the group of people who know it and who practice it daily, that is to say any language is best learnt in its native environment. It does not necessarily mean that no language can be learnt outside its native milieu. In fact, the absence of the native milieu has to be adequately compensated by harder work under guided directions to achieve tangible results. I am sure that this book in hand is one element that can certainly prove useful if the teacher and the taught put their efforts together to exploit it.

I ventured to prepare this book after gaining nearly thirty years experience of teaching both undergraduate and post graduate students coupled with nearly four years stay in the Arab world's cultural and educational hub, the Mecca of Arabic and religious studies, Cairo, the capital of Egypt, as director of Indian Cultural Centre, which position required of me to keep in close touch with masses, and entitled me to interact with bureaucrats and teachers holding high administrative and academic positions which contacts provided me ample opportunities to know and learn as Arabic is ordinarily spoken.

Beside preparing lessons, this book has taken a lot of efforts made over a long period by a good number of people before reaching your hands. My first typist failed to satisfy me, which compelled me to withdraw my book from him. It was required that this book should be by someone who knows Arabic very well, who would do the typing work more for the love of the Arabic language. I was very lucky when one of my own students, Mr. Tahir Helal Ahmad Lari disclosed to me that he knew Arabic-English typing and offered to type this book on the computer for me and he did it. Mr. Lari did this work occasionally at the cost of his own work.

13

be adequate award for his sincere and untiring devotion to this work. However, I still wish to thank him profusely for this work. Thank you Tahir Helal Ahmad Lari. I also consider myself very lucky to have a student-colleague Dr. Rizwanur Rahman who alone typed the most difficult part of this book, that is, the Romanised version of the Arabic texts with improvised symbols. In fact it was this portion which took the most efforts and time for typing and repeated corrections. Thank you Dr. Rizwanur Rahman. Thanks are also due to Mr. Jawed Qamar who accorded help in setting the pages of this book.

I have proofread this book for five times to keep it free from all printing mistakes, however, still I stake no claims that I have been hundred percent successful in achieving this end. There could still be a few typing mistakes but I am sure they can not be of much consequence for the user of this book if he knows the Arabic script and carefully learns the Romanised symbols of the Arabic letters and vowels as each one of these is considered complementary to the other.

I also like to thank Mr. Saniyasnain Khan who agreed to publish this book and my student Mr. Aurang Zeb Azmi who was instrumental in giving me this valuable contact.

Finally, I thank Allah who gave me strength to do this work and this group of sincere and devoted people to help me.

(S.A. RAHMAN)

Arabic Alphabets:

ا ب ت ث ج ح

خ د ذ ر ز س

ش ص ض ط ظ ع

غ ف ق ك ل م

ن ه/ة و ء ى ة

Sun Letters:

ت ث د ذ ر ز س

ش ص ض ط ظ ل ن.

Moon Letters:

ا ب ج ح خ ع غ

ف ق ك م ه و ى.

Romanised symbols of Arabic :

FatHa (above the letter)   ʹ   a

kasra (below the letter)   ˏ   i

damma (above the letter)   ˀ   ö

double fatHa (above the letter)   ˀ   an

double kasra (below the letter)   ˀ   in

double damma (above the letter)   ˀ   ðn

Sökðn   o   or   ˏ

Shaddah   ω

Maddah   ˜

elongative   waw   ð

elongative   alif   ã

elongative   yã   î

List of Abbreviations

s.m.	singular masculine
s.f.	singular feminine
d.m.	dual masculine
d.f.	dual feminine
p.m.	plural masculine
p.f.	plular feminine
pl.	plural
mas.	masculine
fem.	feminine
m.f.	masculine and feminine
s.m. adj	singular masculine adjective
s.f. adi.	singular feminine adjective
imp.	Imperative

Lesson 1

Pronunciation:

أُو	أُ	إِى	إِ	آ	أَ
ð	ö	î	i	ā	aa
بُو	بُ	بِي	بِ	بَا	بَ
bð	bö	bî	bi	bā	ba
تُو	تُ	تِي	تِ	تَا	تَ
tð	tö	tî	ti	tā	ta
ثُو	ثُ	ثِي	ثِ	ثَا	ثَ
Tð	Tö	Tî	Ti	Tā	Ta
جُو	جُ	جِى	جِ	جَا	جَ
jð	jö	jî	ji	jā	ja
حُو	حُ	حِى	حِ	حَا	حَ
Hð	Hö	Hî	Hi	Hā	Ha
خُو	خُ	خِى	خِ	خَا	خَ
Kð	Kö	Kî	Ki	Kā	Ka
دُو	دُ	دِى	دِ	دَا	دَ
dð	dö	dî	di	dā	da
ذُو	ذُ	ذِى	ذِ	ذَا	ذَ
Đð	Đö	Đî	Đi	Đā	Đa

رُو	رُ	رِى	رِ	رَا	رَ
rð	rö	rî	ri	rā	ra
زُو	زُ	زِى	زِ	زا	زَ
zð	zö	zî	zi	zā	za
سُو	سُ	سِى	سِ	سَا	سَ
sð	sö	sî	si	sā	sa
شُو	شُ	شِى	شِ	شَا	شَ
Šð	Šö	Šî	Ši	Šā	Ša
صُو	صُ	صِى	صِ	صَا	صَ
Sð	Sö	Sî	Si	Sā	Sa
ضُو	ضُ	ضِى	ضِ	ضَا	ضَ
dð	dö	dî	di	dā	da
طُو	طُ	طِى	طِ	طَا	طَ
tð	tö	tî	ti	tā	ta
ظُو	ظُ	ظِى	ظِ	ظَا	ظَ
zð	zö	zî	zi	zā	za
عُو	عُ	عِى	عِ	عَا	عَ
a'ð	a'ö	a'î	a'i	a'ā	a'a
غُو	غُ	غِى	غِ	غَا	غَ
ghð	ghö	ghî	ghi	ghā	gha

فُو	فُ	فِى	فِ	فَا	فَ
fð	fö	fî	fi	fā	fa
قُو	قُ	قِى	قِ	قَا	قَ
qð	qö	qî	qi	qā	qa
كُو	كُ	كِى	كِ	كَا	كَ
kð	kö	kî	ki	kā	ka
لُو	لُ	لِى	لِ	لَا	لَ
lð	lö	lî	li	lā	la
مُو	مُ	مِى	مِ	مَا	مَ
mð	mö	mî	mi	mā	ma
نُو	نُ	نِى	نِ	نَا	نَ
nð	nö	nî	ni	nā	na
هُو	هُ	هِى	هِ	هَا	ةَ / هَ
hð	hö	hî	hi	hā	ha
وُو	وُ	وِى	وِ	وَا	وَ
wð	wö	wî	wi	wā	wa
يُو	يُ	يِى	يِ	يَا	يَ
yð	yö	yî	yi	yā	ya
ةُ	ةِ	ةَ	ءُ	ءِ	ءَ
tö	ti	ta	'aö	'ai	'aa

Lesson 2

General Vocabulary

كلمات عامة

English	Transliteration	Arabic
father	'aab	أَبٌ
door	bãb	بَابٌ
slave	a'abd	عَبدٌ
office	mak tab	مكتب
book	ki tãb	كِتَابٌ
library	mak ta ba	مَكتَبةٌ
watchman	Ka fîr	خَفِيرٌ
policepost	maK far	مَخفَرٌ
chicken	fi rãK	فِرَاخٌ
incubation	taf rîK	تَفرِيخٌ
happiness	fa raH	فَرحٌ
pit	Höf ra	حُفرةٌ
camel	ja mal	جَمَلٌ
lesson	dars	دَرسٌ
school	mad ra sa	مَدرَسَة
male	Đa kar	ذَكَرٌ
shrine	maa' bad	مَعبَدٌ
studies	di rã sa	دِرَاسَة

crop	zara'	زَرع
fruit	*Ta* mar	ثَمَرٌ
fullmoon	badr	بَدرٌ
cold	bard	بَرد
kettle	bar rãd	بَرّادٌ
cloak	ri *d*ã'a	رِدَاءٌ
street	Šã ria'	شَارِعٌ
project	maŠ rða'	مَشرُوعٌ
head	ra 'aîs	رَئِيسٌ
condition,bet	Šar†	شَرطٌ
ribbon, tape	Ša rî†	شَرِيطٌ
happiness	sö rðr	سُرُورٌ
shirt	qa mî*S*	قَمِيص
juice	a'a *S*îr	عَصِيرٌ
falcon	*S*aqr	صَقرٌ
palace	qa*S*r	قَصرٌ
cutting	qa*d*m	قَضمٌ
udder	*d*ira'	ضِرعٌ
student	†ã lib	طَالِبٌ
duck	ba††	بَطُّ

23

English	Transliteration	Arabic
cat	qiț ța	قِطَّةٌ
injustice	z̲ölm	ظُلمٌ
oppressor	z̲ā lim	ظَالِم
oppressed	maz̲ lŏm	مَظلُومٌ
worshipper	a'ā bid	عَابِدٌ
manufacturer	S̲ā nia'	صَانِعٌ
past / ancient	ghā bir	غَابِرٌ
dust	ghö bãr	غُبَارٌ
embezzlement	gha ban	غَبنٌ
idea	fik ra	فِكرَة
infidel	kā fir	كَافِرٌ
summer	S̲ayf	صَيفٌ
purity	S̲a fā'a	صَفَاءٌ
pen	qa lam	قَلَمٌ
acceptable	maq bŏl	مَقبُولٌ
driver	sā 'aiq	سَائِقٌ
purse	kîs	كِيسٌ
knife	sik kîn	سِكِّينٌ
fish	sa mak	سَمكٌ
resident	sã kin	سَاكِنٌ

24

English	Transliteration	Arabic
grateful	Šã kir	شَاكِرٌ
gratitude	Šökr	شُكرٌ
night	layl	لَيلٌ
camels	ji mãl	جِمَالٌ
generation	jĩl	جِيلٌ
umbrella	mi zal la	مِظلَّة
fit	lã 'aiq	لَائِقٌ
fitness	li yã qa	لِيَاقَة
brush	mir sam	مِرسَمٌ
painter	ras sãm	رَسَّام
pupil	til mîÐ	تِلمِيذٌ
servant	Kã dim	خَادِم
mohammad	mö Ham mad	مُحمَّدٌ
share/luck	na Sĩb	نَصِيبٌ
representative /delegate	man dðb	مَندُوبٌ
resident	sã kin	سَاكِنٌ
accomodation/ residence	sa kan	سَكن
calm	sö kðn	سُكُون

English	Transliteration	Arabic
tiger	na mir	نَمِرٌ
tigress	na mi ra	نَمِرَة
telephone	hã tif	هَاتِفٌ
day(time)	na hãr	نَهَارٌ
face	wajh	وَجه
river	nahr	نَهرٌ
falling/ descending	hã biŧ	هَابِطٌ
perch	mah biŧ	مَهبِطٌ
paper	wa raq	وَرَقٌ
letter	mak tõb	مَكتوبٌ
peacock	ŧã 'aðs	طَاوُوسٌ
boy	wa lad	وَلَدٌ
valley	wã din	وَادٍ
father	wã lid	وَالِدٌ
hand	yad	يَد
famous	Ša hîr	شَهِيرٌ
chair	kör sî	كُرسِيٌّ
soldier	jön dî	جُندِيٌّ
village	qar ya	قَريَة

26

judge	qā *d*in	قَاضٍ
student	ṭā li ba	طَالَبة
woman	'aim ra 'aa	امرَأة
table	ṭā wi la	طَاوِلَة
phenomenon	ẓā hi ra	ظَاهِرَةٌ
appearance	ẓö hŏr	ظُهُورٌ
get-up/external apperance	maẓ har	مَظْهَرٌ
water	mã'a	مَاءٌ
brother	'aaK	أَخٌ
head	ra'as	رَأسٌ
thing	Šay'a	شَىءٌ
kind	ra 'aðf	رَؤُوفٌ
hundred	mi 'aa	مائَة/ مِئَةٌ

{☆☆☆}

Lesson 3

General vocalubary

كلمات عامة

English	Transliteration	Arabic	Transliteration	Arabic
house	al bay tö	البيت	bay tön	بيت
office	al mak ta bö	المكتب	mak ta bön	مكتب
girl	al bin tö	البنت	bin tön	بنت
boy	al wa la dö	الولد	wa la dön	ولد
fan	al mir wa Ha tö	المروحة	mir wa Ha tön	مروحة
official /officer	al mö waz za fö	الموظف	mö waz za fön	موظف
room	al ghör fa tö	الغرفة	ghör fa tön	غرفة
copy book	al kör rã sa tö	الكراسة	kör rã sa tön	كراسة
slave	al a'ab dö	العبد	a'ab dön	عبد
radio	al miÐ yã a'ö	المذياع	miÐ yã a'ön	مذياع
bread	al Köb zö	الخبز	Köb zön	خبز
elephant	al fi lö	الفيل	fi lön	فيل
dog	al kal bö	الكلب	kal bön	كلب
lock	al qöf lö	القفل	qöf lön	قفل
key	al mif tã Hö	المفتاح	mif tã Hön	مفتاح
university	al jã mi a'a tö	الجامعة	jã mi a'a tön	جامعة
representative/ delegate	al man dõ bö	المندوب	man dõ bön	مندوب

28

servant	al Ḵã di mö	الخادم Ḵã di mön	خادم
telephone	al hã ti fö	الهاتف hã ti fön	هاتف
chair	al kör sî yö	الكرسى kör sî yön	كرسى
banker	al Ṣar rã fö/	الصراف Ṣar rã fön	صراف
	aṢ Ṣar rã fö		
man	al ra jö lö/	الرجل ra jö lön	رجل
	ar ra jö lö		
pilot	al ṭay yã rö/	الطيار ṭay yã rön	طيار
	aṭ ṭay yã rö		
car	al say yã ra tö/	السيارة say yã ra tön	سيارة
	as say yã ra tö		
cupboard	al dð lã bö/	الدولاب dð lã bön	دولاب
	ad dð lã bö		
refrigreator	al Ṭal lã ja tö/	الثلاجة Ṭal lã ja tön	ثلاجة
	aṬ Ṭal lã ja tö		
knife	al sik kî nö/	السكين sik kî nön	سكين
	as sik kî nö		
window	al Šob bã kö/	الشباك Šob bã kön	شباك
	aŠ Šob bã kö		
airplane	al ṭã i ra tö/	الطائرة ṭã 'ai ra tön	طائرة

29

	a† †ã i ra tö		
night	al lay lö	lay lön الليل	ليل
day/	al na hã rö/	na hã rön النهار	نهار
daytime	an na hã rö		
tree	al Ša ja ra tö/	Ša ja ra tön الشجرة	شجرة
	aŠ Ša ja ra tö		
tasty	al la Đî Đö	la Đî Đön اللذيذ	لذيذ
friend	al Sa dî qö/	Sa dî qön الصديق	صديق
	aS Sa dî qö		
cheap	al ra Kî sö/	ra Kî Sön الرخيص	رخيص
	ar ra Kî Sö		
costly	al Ta mî nö/	Ta mî nön الثمين	ثمين
/expensive	aT Ta mî nö		
box /trunk	al Sön dð qö/	Sön dð qön الصندوق	صندوق
	aS Sön dð qö		
companion/	al ra fî qö/	ra fî qön الرفيق	رفيق
friend	ar ra fî qö		
village/	al rî fö/ ar rî fö	rî fön الريف	ريف
countryside			

captain/officer	al *d*ã bi †ö/ a*d* *d*ã bi †ö	الضابط *d*ã bi †ön	ضابط
back	al zah rö/ az zah rö	الظهر zah rön	ظهر
student	al †ã li bö/ a† †ã li bö	الطالب †ã li bön	طالب
bicycle	al dar rã ja tö/ ad dar rã ja tö	الدراجة dar rã ja tön	دراجة
doctor	al †a bî bö/ a† †a bî bö	الطبيب †a bî bön	طبيب
cook	al †ab bã Kö/ a† †ab bã Kö	الطباخ †ab bã Kön	طباخ
blackborad	al sab bð ra tö/ as sab bð ra tö	السبورة sab bð ra tön	سبورة
wolf	al Ði'a bö/ aÐ Ði'a bö	الذئب Ði'a bön	ذئب
cloth	al *T*aw bö/ a*TT*aw bö	الثوب *T*aw bön	ثوب

{☆☆☆}

31

Lesson 4

جموع بعض الكلمات المدروسة
Plurals of some words already done

English	Transliteration	Arabic
doors	'aab wã bön.	أَبوَابٌ
offices	ma kã ti bö	مَكَاتِبُ
books	kö tö bön	كُتُبٌ
students (male)	†öl lã bön	طُلّابٌ
lessons	dö rð sön	دُروسٌ
broadcasters	mö Ðî a'ð na	مُذِيعُونَ
pens	'aaq lã mön	أَقلَامٌ
palaces	qö Sð rön	قُصُورٌ
purses	'aak yã sön	أَكيَاسٌ
shrines	m a'ã bi dö	مَعَابِدُ
cats	qi †a †ön	قِطَطٌ
umbrellas	mi zal lã tön	مظَلَّاتٌ
conditions/bets	Šö rð †ön	شُرُوطٌ
drivers	sã 'ai qö na	سَائِقُونَ
heads (of organization)	rö 'að sã 'aön	رُؤوسَاءُ
cruel people	zã li mð na	ظَالِمُونَ
oppressed people	maz lð mð na	مَظلُومُونَ
shirts	qöm Sã nön	قُمصَانٌ

falcons	_Sö qð rön	صُقُورٌ
letters	ma kã tî bö	مَكَاتِيبُ
rivers	an hã rön	أَنهَارٌ
villages	qö ran	قُرىً
papers	aw rã qön	أَورَاقٌ
representatives/delegates	man dð bð na	مَندُوبُونَ
servants	_Ka da mön	خَدَمٌ
telephones	ha wã ti fo	هَواتِفُ
houses	bö yð tön	بُيُوتٌ
boys	aw lã dön	أَولَادٌ
officials	mö wa_z_ za fð na	مُوَظَّفُونَ
slaves	a'i bã dön	عِبَادٌ
girls	ba nã tön	بَنَاتٌ
chairs	ka rã sî yö	كَرَاسِيُّ
copybooks	kör rã sã tön	كُرَّاسَاتٌ
universities	jã mi a'ã tön	جَامِعَاتٌ
locks	'aaq fã lön	أَقفَالٌ
rooms	ghö rö fã tön	غُرفَاتٌ
keys	ma fã tî _H_ö	مَفَاتِيحُ
dogs	ki lã bön	كِلَابٌ
fans	ma rã wi _H_ö	مَرَاوِحُ

33

English	Transliteration	Arabic
men	ri jã lön	رِجَالٌ
boxes/trunks	Sa nã dî qö	صَنَادِيقُ
pilots	†ay yã rð na	طَيَّارُونَ
friends	'aaS di qã 'aö	أَصدِقَاءُ
windows	Ša bã bî kö	شَبَابِيكُ
airplanes	†ã 'ai rã tön	طَائِرَاتٌ
knives	sa kã kî nö	سَكَاكِينُ
refrigerators	Tal lã jã tön	ثَلّاجَاتٌ
cupboards	da wã lî bö	دَوَالِيبُ
officers/captains	ðöb bã †ön	ضُبّاطٌ
comrades/friends	rö fa qã 'aö	رُفَقَاءُ
bicycles	dar rã jã tön	دَرّاجَاتٌ
doctors	'aa †ib bã 'aö	أَطِبّاءُ
villages	'aar yã fön	أَريَافٌ
bankers	Sar rã fð na	صَرّافُونَ
cooks	†ab bã Kð na	طَبّاخُونَ
faces	wö jð hön	وُجُوهٌ
painters	ras sã mð na	رَسّامُونَ
things	'aaŠ yã 'aö	أَشيَاءُ
judges	qö ðã tön	قُضَاةٌ
external appearances	za wã hi rö	ظَوَاهِرُ

34

cars	say yã rã tön	سَيَّارَاتٌ
blackboards	sab bð rã tön	سَبُّوراتٌ
schools	ma dã ri sö	مَدَارِسُ
studies	di rã sã tön	بِرَاسَاتٌ
streets	Ša wã ri a'ö	شَوَرِاعُ
infidels	köf fã rön	كُفَّارٌ
brothers	'ai<u>K</u> wã tön	إِخْوَةٌ
(girl)students	†ã li bã tön	طَالِبَاتٌ
tables	†ã wi lã tön	طَاوِلَاتٌ
women	ni sã 'aön	نِسَاءٌ
pupils	ta lã mî Ðö	تَلَامِيذُ
residents/inmates	sök kã nön	سُكَّانٌ
medicines/drugs	ad wi ya tön	أَدوِيَةٌ
wolves	Ði 'aã bön	ذِئَابٌ
cltothes	'aa*T* wã bön	أَثوَابٌ
soldiers	jö nð dön	جُنُودٌ
tigers	'aan mã rön	أَنمَارٌ
heads	rö 'að sön	رُؤوسٌ
peacocks	†a wã wî sö	طَوَاوِيسُ

{☆ ☆ ☆}

35

Lesson 5

Useful vocabulary		كلمات مفيدة
father	'aa bön (wã li dön)	أبٌ (والد)
mother	'aöm mön (wã li da tön)	أمٌّ (والدة)
husband	zaw jön	زَوجٌ
wife	zaw ja tön	زَوجةٌ
son	'aib nön	اِبنٌ
daughter	bin tön	بنتٌ
brother	'aa Kön	أخٌ
sister	'aöK tön	أختٌ
full brother	Ša qî qön	شَقيقٌ
full sister	Ša qî qa tön	شَقيقةٌ
grandfather	jad dön	جَدٌّ
grandmother	jad da tön	جَدَّةٌ
uncle (from father's side)	a'am mön	عَمٌّ
aunty (from father's side)	a'am ma tön	عَمَّةٌ
uncle (from mother's side)	Kã lön	خَالٌ
aunty (from mother's side)	Kã la tön	خَالةٌ
head	ra'a sön	رَأسٌ
forehead	jab ha tön	جَبَهةٌ

36

eye	a'ay nön	عَينٌ
nose	'aan fön	أنفٌ
cheek	Kad dön	خَدٌ
lip	Ša fa tön	شَفةٌ
mouth	fa mön	فَمٌ
tongue	li sã nön	لِسَانٌ
tooth	sin nön	سن
neck	a'ö nö qön	عُنُقٌ
chest	Sad rön	صَدرٌ
belly(abdomen)	ba† nön	بَطنٌ
back	zah rön	ظَهرٌ
arm	sã a'i dön	سَاعِدٌ
wrist	mia' Sa mön	مِعصَمٌ
finger	'aiS ba a'ön	إِصبَعٌ
palm	kaf fön	كَفٌ
heart	qal bön	قَلبٌ
shank	sã qön	سَاقٌ
foot	qa da mön	قَدمٌ
ankle	kaa' bön	كَعبٌ
navel	sör ra tön	سُرةٌ

hand	ya dön	يَدٌ
eyebrow	_H_ã ji bön	حَاجِبٌ
shoulder	ka ti fön	كَتِفٌ
nail	_z_ö fö rön	ظُفُرٌ
knee	rök ba tön	رُكْبَةٌ
hair	Šaa' rön	شَعَرٌ
leg	rij lön	رِجْلٌ
nostril	_K_ay Šð mön	خَيْشُومٌ
chin	Ði qa nön	ذِقَنٌ
thigh	fa _K_i Ðön	فَخِذ
waist	_K_i_S_ rön	خِصْرٌ
forehead	ja bî nön	جَبِينٌ
teacher/professor	'aös tã Ðön	أُسْتَاذٌ
student (boy)	†ã li bön	طَالِبٌ
student (girl)	†ã li ba tön	طَالِبَةٌ
pupil	til mî Ðön	تِلْمِيذٌ
peon/office attendant	far rã Šön	فَرَّاشٌ
principal/dean	a'a mî dön	عَمِيدٌ
headmaster	nã _z_i rön	نَاظِرٌ
teacher	mö dar ri sön	مُدَرِّسٌ

38

instructor	mö a'al li mön	مُعَلِّم
sweeper	kan nã sön	كَنَّاس
writer/clerk	kã ti bön	كَاتِب
registrar	mö saj ji lön	مُسَجِّل
college/faculty	köl lî ya tön	كُلِّية
school	mad ra sa tön	مَدرَسة
university	jã mi a'a tön	جَامِعَة
book	ki tã bön	كتَاب
office	mak ta bön	مَكتَب
class/classroom	faS̲ lön	فَصل
water closet	daw ra töl mi yã hi	دَورَةُ المِيَاه
latrine,toilet	mir H̱ã d̲ön	مِرحَاض
field/ground	may dã nön	مَيدَان
hall	qã a'a tön	قَاعة
boundary wall	sð rön	سُور
wall	H̱ã 'ai †ön	حَائِط
garden	H̱a dî qa tön	حَديقَة
gardener	bös tã nî yön	بُستَانِی
trees	aŠ jã rön	أشجَار
plants	na bã tã tön	نَبَاتَات

39

water tank	Sih rî jön	صِهْرِيجٌ
tap	Ha na fî ya tön	حَنَفِيَّةٌ
pipe	Kör †ð mön	خُرْطُومٌ
inkpot	da wã tön	دَوَاةٌ
erazor	mim Hã tön	مِمْحَاةٌ
copybook	kör rã sa tön	كُرَّاسَةٌ
blackboard	sab bð ra tön	سَبُّورَةٌ
chalk stick	†a bã $Š$î rö	طَبَاشِيرُ
pen	qa la mön	قَلَمٌ
chair	kör sî yön	كُرسِيٌّ
table	†ã wi la tön	طَاوِلَةٌ
floor	'aar dî ya tön	أَرْضِيَّةٌ
floor spread	far $Š$ön	فَرشٌ
furniture	'aa Tã Tön	أَثَاثٌ
carpet	saj jã dön	سَجَّادٌ

{☆☆☆}

Lesson 6

Demonstrative pronouns

أسماء الاشارة

	faminine		masculine	
This	hã Đi hi	هذه	hã Đã	هذا
These(two)	hã tã ni	هاتان	hã Đã ni	هذان
These(all)	ha 'að lã 'ai	هؤلاء	ha 'að lã 'ai	هولاء
That	til ka	تلك	Đã li ka	ذلك
Those(two)	tã ni ka	تانك	Đã ni ka	ذانك
Those(all)	'að lã 'ai ka	اولئك	'að lã 'ai ka	اولئك

nominative personal pronoun

الضمائر المنفصلة

	feminine			masculine	
She	hi ya	هى	he	hö wa	هو
They(two)	hö mã	هما	they(two)	hö mã	هما
They(all)	hön na	هن	they(all)	höm	هـم
You	'aan ti	أنت	you	'aan ta	أنت
You(two)	'aantömã	أنتما	you(two)	'aantömã	أنتما
You(all)	'aantön na	أنتن	you(all)	'aan töm	أنتم
We(m.f.)	naHnö	نحن	I(m.f)	'aa nã	أنا

41

English	Transliteration	Arabic
This is a book.	hã Ðã ki tã bön	هَذَا كِتَابٌ.
These are (two) books.	hã Ðã ni ki tã bã ni	هَذَانِ كِتَابَانِ.
These are books.	hã Ði hi kö tö bön	هٰذِهِ كُتُبٌ.
This is a boy.	hã Ðã wa la dön	هٰذَا وَلَدٌ.
These are (two) boys.	hã Ðã ni wa la dã ni	هٰذَانِ وَلَدَانِ.
These are boys.	ha 'að lã 'ai 'aw lã dön	هٰؤُلَاءِ أَوْلَادٌ.
This is a copybook.	hã Ði hi kör rã sa tön	هٰذِهِ كُرَّاسَةٌ.
These are (two) copybooks.	hã tã ni kör rã sa tã ni	هَاتَانِ كُرَاسَتَانِ.
These are copybooks.	hã Ðihi kör rã sã tön	هٰذِهِ كُرَّاسَاتٌ.
This is a girl.	hã Ði hi bin tön	هٰذِهِ بِنتٌ.
These are (two) girls.	hã tã ni bin tã ni	هَاتَانِ بِنتَانِ.
These are girls.	ha 'að lã 'ai ba nã tön	هٰؤُلَاءِ بَنَاتٌ.
That is a book.	Ðã li ka ki tã bön	ذٰلِك كِتَابٌ.
Those are (two) books.	Ðã ni ka ki tã bã ni	ذَانِك كِتَابَانِ.
Those are books.	til ka kö tö bön	تِلك كُتُبٌ.
That is a boy.	Ðã li ka wa la dön	ذٰلِك وَلَدٌ.
Those are (two) boys.	Ðã ni ka wal dã ni	ذَانِك وَلَدَانِ.
Those are boys.	'að lã 'ai ka 'aw lã dön	أُولَئِك أَوْلَادٌ.
That is a copybook.	til ka kör rã sa tön	تِلك كُرَّاسَةٌ.
Those are	tã ni ka	تَانِك

42

English	Transliteration	Arabic
(two) copybooks.	kör rã sa tã ni	كُرَّاسَتَانِ.
Those are copybooks.	til ka kör rã sã tön	تِلك كُرَّاسَاتُ.
That is a girl.	til ka bin tön	تِلك بِنتُ.
Those are (two) girls.	tã ni ka bin tã ni	تَانِك بِنتَانِ.
Those are girls.	'að lã 'ai ka ba nã tön	أُولئِك بَنَاتُ.
He is a teacher.	hö wa mö dar ri sön	هُو مُدَرِّسُ.
They are	hö mã	هُمَا
(two) teachers.	mö dar ri sã ni	مُدَرِّسَانِ.
They are teachers.	höm mö dar ri sỏ na	هُم مُدَرِّسُونَ.
She is a teacher	hi ya mö dar ri sa tön	هِى مُدَرِّسِةٌ.
They are (two)	hö mã	هُمَا
teachers (lady).	mö dar ri sa tã ni	مُدَرِّسَتَانِ.
They are	hön na	هُنَّ
teachers (lady).	mö dar ri sã tön	مُدَرِّسَاتُ.
You are a teacher. (s.m.)	'aan ta mö dar ri sön	أَنتَ مُدَرِّسُ.
You are (two)	'aan tö mã	أَنتُمَا
teachers. (d.m.)	mö dar ri sã ni	مُدَرِّسَان.
You are	'aan töm	أَنتم
teachers. (p.m.)	mö dar ri sỏ na	مُدَرِّسُون.
I am a teacher. (s.m.)	'aa nã mö dar ri sön	أَنا مدرس.
I am a teacher. (s.f.)	'aa nã mö dar ri sa tön	أَنامُدَرِّسِةٌ.

43

English	Transliteration	Arabic
We are teachers. (p.m.)	naH nö mö dar ri sŏ na	نحن مُدَرِّسُون.
We are teachers. (p.f.)	naH nö mö dar ri sã tön	نَحنُ مُدَرِّسَات.
We are (two) teachers. (d.m)	naH nö mö dar ri sã ni	نَحنُ مُدَرِّسَان.
We are (two) teachers. (d.f)	naH nö mö dar ri sa tã ni	نَحنُ مُدَرِّسَتَانِ.
Are you a teacher?	hal 'aan ta mö dar ri sön	هَل أنتَ مُدَرِّسٌ؟
Yes, I am a teacher.	na a'am, 'aa nã mö dar ri sön	نَعَم، أَنَا مُدَرِّسٌ.
And who are you?	wa man 'aan ta	وَمَن أنتَ؟
I am also a teacher.	'aa nã mö dar ri sön 'aay dan	أَنَا مُدَرِّسٌ أيضاً.
Are you a teacher?	hal 'aan ti mö dar ri sa tön	هَل أنتِ مُدَرِّسَةٌ؟
Yes,	na a'am,	نَعَم،
I am a teacher.	'aa nã mö dar ri sa tön	أَنَا مُدَرِّسَةٌ.
And who is she?	wa man hi ya	وَمَن هِي؟
She is also a teacher.	hi ya mö dar ri sa tön	هِي مُدَرِّسَةٌ

	'aay *d*an	أيضا
Is he a teacher?	hal hö wa mö da r risön	هَل هُو مُدَرِّسٌ؟
Yes	na a'am	نَعَم
he is a teacher.	hö wa mö dar ri sön	هُو مُدَرِّسٌ.
Are you	hal 'aan töm	هَل أنتُم
teachers?	mö dar ri sŏ na	مُدَرِّسُونَ.
Yes,	na a'am,	نَعَم،
we are teachers.	na*H* nö mö dar ri sŏ na	نَحنَ مُدَرِّسُونَ.
Who are you.?	ma 'aan tön na	مَن أنتُنَّ؟
We are also	na*H* nömö dar ri sã	نَحنُ مُدَرِّسَاتُ
teachers .	tön 'aay *d*an	أيضاً.
Who are they?	man höm	مَن هُم ؟
They are teachers.	höm mö dar ri sŏ na	هُم مُدَرِّسُونَ.
Are they	hal hön na	هَل هَنَّ
also	mö dar ri sã tön	مُدَرِّسَاتُ
teachers?	'aay *d*an	أيضاً؟
Yes.	na a'am	نَعَم
They are teachers.	hön na mö dar ri sã tön	هُنَّ مُدَرِّسَاتُ.

Lesson 7

General Conversation		محادثة عامة
Visitor:	az zã 'air:	اَلزَّائِر:
Good morning	Sa bã Hal Kayr,	صَبَاحَ الخَير
sir.	yã say yi dî.	يَاسَيِّدى.
Office employee:	mö waz za föl mak tab:	مُوَظَّفُ المَكتَب:
Good morning.	Sa bã Hal Kayr.	صَبَاحَ الخَير.
How do you do?	kay fal Hãl?	كَيفَ الحَال ؟
Visitor:	az zã 'air:	اَلزَّائِر:
Good,	ṭay yib,	طَيِّب،
and how do you do?	wa kay fan ta?	وَكَيفَ اَنتَ؟
Office employee:	mö waz za föl mak tab:	مُوَظَّف المَكتَب:
I am good,	'aa nã bi Kayr,	أَنَا بخَير،
all praise be to Allah.	wal Ham dö lil lãh.	وَالحَمدُلِلَّه.
Who are you?	man 'aan ta?	مَن أَنتَ؟
Visitor:	az zã 'air:	اَلزَّائِر:
I am an engineer.	'aa nã mö han dis.	أَنَا مُهندِس.
My name is Jameel.	'ais mî ja mîl.	اسمى جَمِيل.
and this is	wa hã Ðã	وَهَذَا
my friend Shankar.	Sa dî qî Šan kar.	صَدِيقى شَنكَر.

He is my colleague	hö wa za mî lî	هُوَ زَميلى
at work.	fil a'a mal.	فى العَمَل.
Office employee:	mö waz za föl mak tab:	مُوَظَّفُ المَكتَب:
Where are you from?	min 'aay na 'aan töm?	مِن أينَ أنتُم؟
Visitor:	az zã 'air:	اَلزَائِر:
we are from India.	naH nö mi nal hind.	نَحنُ مِن الهِند.
We have come now	Ha dar nal 'aã na	حَضَرنَا الآن
to meet	li mö qã ba la ti	لِمُقابَلَةِ
the minister of educatoin.	wa zîr at taa' lîm.	وَزِيرِالتَعلِيم.
Office employee:	mö waz za föl maktab:	مُوَظَّفُ المَكتَب:
Sorry,	'aã sif.	آسِف.
the minister	al wa zîr	الوَزِير
is busy	maŠ ghöl	مَشغُول
now.	al 'aã na.	الآن.
Visitor:	az zã 'air;	اَلزَائِر:
Tell us	qöl la nã	قُل لَنَا
please,	min fad lik	مِن فَضلِك
when will	ma tã ya kön	مَتىٰ يَكُونُ
the minister be free?	al wa zîr fã di yan?	الوَزِيرُفَاضِنيا؟
Office employee:	mö waz za föl maktab:	مُوَظَّفُ المَكتَب:

47

English	Transliteration	Arabic
Tomorrow	gha dan	غَداً
in the morning.	Sa bã Han.	صَبَاحاً.
Visitor:	az zã 'air:	اَلزَائِر:
Good, we will come	tay yib‹ na jî 'aö	طَيِّب ، نجيء
tomorrow morning.	gha dan Sa bã Han.	غداً صباحاً.
Please	min fadlik	مِن فَضلِك
fix our appointment	Had did maw a'i da nã	حَدِّد موعدنا
with him for tomorrow.	ma a'a hö gha dan.	مَعَه غداً.
Office employee:	mö waz za föl maktab:	مُوَظَّفُ المَكتَب:
Good.	†ay yib.	طَيِّب.
Tomorrw morning at	gha dan fis sã a'a til	غداًفِى السَاعَةِ
10 O'clock	a'ã Ši ra	العَاشِرَةِ
if God so willing.	'ain Šã 'aal lah.	إن شَاءَ اللَّه.
Thanks a lot.	Šök ran ja zîlan.	شُكراًجَزِيلاً.
See you,	'ai lal li qã 'a	إلى اللِقَاءِ
tomorrow morning	gha dan Sa bã Han.	غداًصباحاً.

Exercise: التمرين:

Question(1) السؤال(١)

Who goes	man yaÐ hab	مَن يَذهَبُ
to meet the	li mö qã ba lat	لِمُقَابَلَةِ
minister of education?	wa zîr 'aat taa' lîm?	وَزِيرِالتَعلِيم؟

Answer الجواب

Jameel goes	ja mîl yaÐ hab	جَمِيلٌ يَذهَبُ
to meet the	li mö qã ba lat	لِمُقَابَلَةِ
minister of educatiion.	wa zîr at taa' lîm.	وَزِيرِالتَعلِيم.

Question(2) السوال(٢)

| Who was with him? | man kã na ma a'a hö? | مَن كَانَ مَعَهُ ؟ |

Answer الجواب

| There was with him | kã na ma a'a hö | كَانَ مَعَهُ |
| his friend Shanker. | Sa dî qö hö Šan kar. | صَدِيقُهُ شنكر. |

Question(3) السؤال(٣)

| Is Jameel engineer? | hal ja mîl mö han dis? | هَل جَمِيلٌ مُهندِسٌ؟ |

Answer الجواب

| Yes, | na a'am, | نَعَم، |
| he is engineer. | hö wa mö han dis | هُو مُهَندِسٌ. |

Question(4) السؤال (٤)

Was the minister busy.	hal kã nal wa zî rö maŠ ghð lan?	هَل كَانَ الوَزِير مَشغُولاً؟
Answer		الجواب
Yes, the minister was busy.	na a'am, kã nal wazî rö maŠ ghð lan.	نَعَم ، كَانَ الوَزِير مَشغُولاً.
Question(5)		السؤال(٥)
When will the minister be free?	ma tã ya kð nöl wa zir fa di yan?	مَتىٰ يَكُونُ الوَزِيرُ فَاضِياً؟
Answer		الجواب
The minister will be free in the morning the next day.	ya kð nöl wa zîr fã di yan fiṢ Ṣa bã Hi fil yaw mit tã lî.	يكون الوزير فاضيا في الصباح في اليوم التالي.

《☆☆☆》

50

Lesson 8

General Convesation

مُحَادَثَةٌ عَامَّةٌ

Shanker in Cairo	Šan kar fil qã hi ra	شَنكرفِى القَاهِرَة
in Egypt	fîmi Sr.	فِى مِصر.
Shanker to way farer :	Šan kar li 'aib ni sa bîl:	شَنكر لابنِ سَبِيل:
sir?	say yi dî?	سَيِّدى؟
Wayfarer:	'aib nös sa bîl	إبنُ السَّبِيل :
Yes sir,	na a'am yã say yi dî.	نَعَم، يَاسَيِّدى.
Shanker: I am	Šan kar: 'aa nã	شَنكَر :أَنَا
new in Cairo .	ja dîd fil qã hi rã.	جَدِيدٌفِى القَاهِرَة.
Wayfarer:	'aib nös sa bîl:	إبنُ السَبِيل:
Welcome	'aah lan wa sah lan	أهلاً وسـهلاً
my friend.	yã Sa dî qî.	يَاصَدِيقِى .
Are you	hal 'aan ta	هَل أنتَ
Indian?	hin dî?	هِندىٌ؟
Shanker: yes,	Šan kar: na a'am,	شَنكر: نَعَم ،
sir,	yã say yi dî	يا سيدى ،
I am Indian .	'aa nã hin dî.	أ نَاهِندِى.
Wayfarer:	'aib nös sa bîl:	ابنُ السَبِيل :
What do you want?	mã Ðã tö rîd?	مَاذَا تُرِيدُ ؟

51

English	Transliteration	Arabic
Shanker: I want	Šan kar: 'aö rîd	شَنكر: أُرِيدُ
to go	'aaÐ hab 'ai lã	أَذهَبُ الى
to the post office.	mak ta bil ba rîd.	مَكتَب البَرِيد.
Wayfarer:	'aib nös sa bîl:	ابنُ السَبِيل:
The Central	mak ta böl ba rîd	مَكتَبُ البَرِيد
Post Office	al mar ka zî	المَركَزِى
is in the street	fiŠ Šã ria'	فِى الشَارِع
on your right.	a'a lã ya mînik	عَلى يَمِينِك.
Shanker: Thanks.	Šan kar: Šök ran	شَنكر: شُكراً.
Wayfarer:	'aib nös sa bîl:	ابنُ السَبِيل:
Tell me	qöl lî min	قُل لِى مِن
please	fad lik	فَضلِك
sir,	yã say yi dî,	يَاسَيِدى ،
why have you come	li mã Ðã ji'a ta	لِمَاذَاجِئتَ
to Egypt?	'ai lã miSr?	إِلى مِصر؟
Shanker: sir,	Šan kar: say yi dî	شَنكر:سَيِّدِى ،
I am an engineer.	'aa nã mö han dis	أَنَا مُهندِس.
I came to	qa dim tö 'ai lã	قَدِمتُ الى
Egypt on	miSr fî	مِصرفِى
an official	mö him ma tin	مُهِمَّةٍ

work.	ras mî ya tin.	رَسَمِيةٍ.
Wayfarer:	'aib nös sa bîl:	ابنُ السَبِيل :
Where do you stay	'aay na tö qî mö	اينَ تُقيمُ
here?	hö nã?	هنا؟
Shanker: I	Šan kar: 'aa nã	شَنكر: أنا
stay	'aö qî mö	ُأقِيم
in hotel	fî fön döq	فِى فُندق
Sheraton.	Šî rã tõn.	شيراتون.
Wayfarer:	'aib nös sa bîl:	ابنُ السَبِيل :
My name is	'ais mî	اسمى
Abdullah.	a'ab döl lãh.	عَبدُالله.
Let us go to	fal naÐ hab 'ai lã	فَلنَذهَب إلى
a restaurant	ma† a'am	مَطعَم
and drink tea.	wa naŠ ra biŠ Šãy.	وَنَشرَب الشَاى.
Shanker: I don,t want	Šan kar: lã 'aö rîd	شَنكر:ٰلاأُرِيدُ
tea now.	'aaŠ Šã y al 'aã na.	الشَاى الآن .
Take my address,	KöÐ a'ön wã nî,	خُذ عُنوَانى ،
Hotel Sheraton.	fön döq Šî rã tõn.	فندق شيراتون.
My room No is	raq mö ghör fa tî	رَقمُ غُرفَتى
one hundred.	mi 'aa.	مِئَة.

53

English	Transliteration	Arabic
We will meet	nal ta qî	نَلتَقِى
tomorrow in	gha dan fî	غداً فِى
my room at	ghör fa tî fî	غُرفَتِى فِى
5	as sã a'a til Kã mi sa	السَّاعَةِ الخَامِسَةِ
P.M.	ma sã 'aan.	مَسَاءً.
Wayfarer:	'aib nös sa bîl	ابنُ السَّبِيل :
Good,	ťay yib,	طَيِّبٌ،
we, will meet	nal ta qî	نَلتَقِى
tomorrow	gha dan	غَداً
if God so willing,	'ain Šã 'aal lãh	إن شَاءَ اللَّهِ ،
A Dieu,	ma a'as sa lã ma	مع السلامة .
Shanker:	Šan kar:	شَنكر:
A Dieu,	ma a'as sa lã ma,	مَعَ السَّلَامَة،
see you.	'ai lal li qã'a	الى اللِقَاءِ.

Exercise

التمرين

Question (1)		السؤال (١)
Who is Shanker?	man hö wa Šan kar?	مَن هُو شَنكَر؟
Answer		الجواب
Shanker is an engineer	Šan kar mö han dis	شَنكر مُهندس

English	Transliteration	Arabic
and he is Indian.	wa hö wa hin dî.	وهُو هِندى .
Question (2)		السؤال (٢)
Where was	'aay na kãn na	أينَ كَانَ
Shanker?	Šan kar?	شَنكَر؟
Answer		الجواب
Shanker was	Šan kar kã na	شَنكَر كَانَ
in Cairo.	fil qã hi rã	فِى القَاهِرَة .
Question(3)		السؤال(٣)
Where does	'aay na yö qî mö	أينَ يُقِيمُ
Shanker stay?	Šan kar?	شنكر؟
Answer		الجواب
Shanker stays in	Šan kar yö qî mö fî	شَنكَر يُقِيم فِى
hotel Sheraton.	fön döq Ši rã ton.	فُندق شيراتون .
Question (4)		السوال(٤)
Did Shanker	hal Ða ha ba	هَل ذَهَبَ
go	Šan kar	شَنكَر
with the wayfarer?	ma a'ab nis sa bîl?	مَعَ ابن السبيل ؟
Answer		الجواب
No Shanker	lã, Šan kar	لا ، شنكر
did not go	lam yaÐ hab	لم يذهب

with the wayfarer.	ma a'ab nis sa bîl.	مع ابن السبيل
Question (5)		السؤال(٥)
Did you go	hal Ða hab ta	هَل ذَهَبتَ
to Cairo?	'ai lal qã hi ra?	إلَى القَاهِرَة ؟
Answer		الجواب
No, I did not go	lã, lam 'aaÐ hab	لَا، لَم أذهَب
to Cario	'ai lal qã hi ra	الى القَاهِرَة
till now.	lil 'aãn.	لِلآن .

❰☆☆☆❱

General Conversatoin — محادثة عامة

English	Transliteration	Arabic
Cold day		يَومٌ بَارِدٌ
It was	kã nal yaw mö	كَانَ اليَومُ
a very cold day .	bã ri dan jid dan.	بَارِدًا جِدًّا.
We had	kã na la nã	كَانَ لَنَا
lesson	ad dar sö	الدَّرسُ
in the evening .	fil ma sã 'ai.	فِى المَسَاءِ.
The teacher entered	da Ka lal 'aös tã Đö	دَخَلَ الأُستَاذُ
the class.	aS Saf fa.	الصَّفَّ.
He was wearing	kã na yal ba sö	كَانَ يَلبَسُ
woollen clothes.	ma lã bi sa Sö fî ya.	مَلَابِسَ صُوفِيَّةً.
The teacher said;	qã lal 'aös ta Đö:	قَالَ الأُستَاذُ :
Open your book,	'aif ta Hil ki tãb,	إفتح الكتابَ،
O , Adil .	yã a'ã dil.	يَا عَادِلُ .
Open	'aif ta Hö	إفتَحُوا
your books,	kö tö ba köm	كُتُبَكُم
O , boys.	yã 'aw lãd .	يَاأَولَادُ.
The teacher began	'aa Ka Đal 'aös tã Đö	أَخَذَ الأُستَاذُ
to teach the lesson	yö dar ri söd dar sa	يُدَرِّسُ الدَّرسَ

English	Transliteration	Arabic
and wrote the	wa ka ta bal ka li mã	وَكَتَبَ الكَلِمَاتِ
difficult words	tiS Saa' ba ta	الصَعبَةَ
on the blackboard.	a'a las sab bð ra ti.	عَلَىٰ السَبُّورَةِ .
The students began	'aa Ka Ðaṭ ṭöl lã bö	أَخَذَ الطُّلَّابُ
to write meanings	yak tö bð nal ma a'ã ni	يَكتُبونَ المَعَانِى
in their copybooks	fî kör rã sã ti him .	فِى كُرَّاسَاتهِمِ .
The teacher asked	sa 'aa lal 'aös tã Ðö	سَأَلَ الأُستَاذُ
a(girl)student :	ṭã li ba tan:	طَالِبَةً :
where is your copy,	'aay na kör rã sã töki	أَينَ كُرّاسَتُكِ
miss?	yã 'aã ni sa?	يَا آنِسَةُ ؟
Here is my copybook,	hö nã kör rã sa tî	هُنَا كُرّاسَتِى
sir.	yã say yi dî.	يَاسَيِّدِى .
Good.	ṭay yib.	طَيِّبٌ
Open your copybook	'aif ta Hî kör rã sa tak	إفتَحِى كُرّاسَتَك
and write	wak tö bî	وَاكتُبِى
these words	hã Ði hil ka li mã ti	هذِه الكَلِمَاتِ
with their meanings.	ma a'a ma a'ã nî hã	مَعَ مَعَانِيهَا .
Why do you write	li mã Ðã tak tö bö	لِمَاذَاتَكتُبُ
on the book,	a'a lal ki tã bi	عَلَىٰ الكِتَابِ
Adil?	yã a'ã dil?	يَا عَادِلُ ؟

58

English	Transliteration	Arabic
Don't write	lã tak töb	لَاتَكتُبْ
on the book.	a'a lal ki tãb.	عَلىٰ الكِتَابِ.
It/ this is	hã Ði hi	هذِه
a bad habit.	a'ã da tönsay yi'aatön.	عَادةٌ سَيِّئَةٌ.
Don't write	lã tak tö bð	لَاتَكتُبُوا
on the books,	a'a lal kö tö bi	عَلىٰ الكُتُبِ
boys	yã 'aw lad.	يَا اولَادُ.
Don't write	lã tak tö bî	لَاتَكتُبِى
on the book,	a'a lal ki tã bi	عَلىٰ الكِتَابِ
miss.	yã 'aã ni sa.	يَاآنسَةُ .
Don't write	lã tak töb na	لَاتَكتُبنَ
on the books,	a'a lal kö tö bi	عَلىٰ الكُتُبِ
girls.	yã ba nã tö.	يَابَنَاتُ.
The bell rang	ran nal ja ra sö	رَنَّ الجَرسُ
and the lesson ended.	wan ta had dar sö.	وَانتَهَى الدَّرسُ.
The teacher said:	wa qã lal 'aös tã Ðö:	وَقَالَ الأُستَاذُ
Good, see you	†ay yib, 'ai lal li qã i	طَيِّبٌ ، إلىٰ اللِقَاءِ
tomorrow.	gha dan.	غَداً.
Then he left	fa Ka ra ja	فَخَرَجَ
and we left	wa Ka raj nã	وَخَرَجنَا
with him.	ma a'a hö.	مَعَه .

59

Exercise		التمرين
Question(1)		السؤال (١)
How	kay fa	كَيفَ
was the day?	kã nal yaw mö?	كَانَ اليَومُ ؟
Answer		الجواب
The day was	kã nal yaw mö	كَانَ اليَومُ
very cold.	bã ri dan jid dan.	بَارِداً جِدًّا.
Question (2)		السؤال (٢)
Who entered the	man da Ka laS	مَن دَخَلَ
class?	Saf fa?	الصّف ؟
Answer		الجواب
The teacher entered	da Ka lal 'aös tã DöS	دَخَلَ الأُستَاذُ
the class .	Saf fa.	الصَّف
Question (3)		السؤال(٣)
What was	mã Đã kã na	مَاذَا كَانَ
the teacher wearing?	yal ba söl 'aös tã Đö?	يَلبَسُ الأُستَاذُ ؟
Answer		الجواب
The teacher was	kã nal 'aös ta Đö	كَانَ الأُستَاذُ
wearing	yal ba sö	يَلبَسُ

60

English	Transliteration	Arabic
woollen clothes.	ma lã bi sa <u>S</u>ŏ fî ya.	مَلَابِسَ صُوفِيَّةً.
Question (4)		السؤال (٤)
What did the	mã Ðã sa 'aa lal	مَاذَا سَأَلَ
teacher ask	'aös tã Ðö	الأُستَاذُ
a (girl) student?	†ã li ba tan?	طَالِبَةً؟
Answer		الجواب
The teacher asked	sa 'aa lal 'aös tã Ðö	سَأَلَ الأُستَاذُ
a (girl) student :	†ã li ba tan,	طَالِبَةً :
Where is your copybook,	'aay na kör rã sa tök	أَينَ كُرَّاسَتُكِ
miss?	yã 'aã ni sa?	يَاآنِسَةُ؟
Question (5)		السؤال (٥)
What did The	mã Ðã qã la ti†	مَاذَاقَالَت
(girl) student say?	†ã li ba tö?	الطَّالِبَةُ ؟
Answer		الجواب
The (girl) student	qã la ti† †ã li ba tö:	قَالَت الطَّالِبَةُ :
said : Here is my copybook,	hö nã kör rã sa tî	هُنَا كُرَّاسَتِى
sir.	yã say yi dî.	يَاسَيِّدِى.

⟨☆☆☆⟩

61

Lesson 10

Miscellaneous Vocabulary

كَلِمَاتٌ مُتَفَرِّقَةٌ

English	Transliteration	Arabic
How	kay fa /kayf	كَيْفَ
How many / how much	kam	كَمْ
When	ma tã	مَتَى
Where	'aay na	أَيْنَ
Who	man	مِنْ
What	mã Đã /mã	مَاذَا /ما
Welcome	ah lan wa sah lan	أَهْلاً وَسَهْلاً
to you	bi köm	بِكُمْ
Welcome to you	ah lan bi köm	أَهْلاً بِكُم
Yes	na a'am	نَعَم
No	lã	لَا
Please	min faḍ lik	مِنْ فَضْلِك
Thanks / thank you	Šök ran	شُكْراً
Yes, please	na a'am, min faḍ lik	نَعَم ، مِنْ فَضْلِك
What is the time	ka mis sã a'a	كَمِ السَّاعَة
How much is the	ka mil	كَمِ
distance	ma sã fa	الْمَسَافَة

What is that	mã Ðã lik	مَاذلك
What do you want?	mã Ðã tö rîd	مَاذَاتُريد
What should I do	mã Ðã 'aaf a'al	مَاذَا أُفْعَل
Where can	'aay na mömkin	أينَ مُمْكِن
I find...	'aa jid	أجِدُ...
Can you help	hal mömkin	هَلُ مُمْكِن
me in...	tö sã a'id nî fî...	تُسَاعِدُنى فى...
Do you know Arabic	hal taa' rif a'a ra bî	هَلُ تَعْرِفُ عَرَبى
French	fö ran sî	فُرَنسى
German	'aal mã nî	الَمَانى
Japanese	yã bã nî	يَابَانى
Chinese	S̲î nî	صِينى
Persian	fã ri sî	فَارسى
How much is it?	bi kam hã Ðã	بِكَم هذا
Is it ready ?	hal hã Ðã jã hiz	هَلُ هذا جَاهِز
Can you guide me	hal tör Ši dö nî	هَلُ تُرشِدُنى
to ...road/street	a'a lã Šã ria'...	علىٰ شَارِع...
Where do you live?	'aay na tas kön?	أينَ تَسُكُن ؟
I live in	'aas kön fî	أسُكُن فى
R.K. Puram.	R.K bð rãm.	ر.ك، بورام ؟

63

English	Transliteration	Arabic
What is your age?/ How old are you?	kam a'öm rök?	كَم عُمرُك؟
I am twenty years old.	a'öm rî a'iŠ rð na sa na.	عُمرِى عِشرُون سِنة.
Where are you from?	min 'aay na 'aan ta?	مِن أينَ أنتَ؟
I am from Varanasi.	'aa nã min fã rã nã sî.	أنَا مِنْ فَارَاناسِى.
Where do you stay here?	'aay na 'aan ta mö qîm hö nã?	أينَ أنتَ مُقيمٌ هنا؟
I stay with a friend of mine.	'aa nã mö qîm ma a'a Sa dîqin lî.	أنَا مُقِيمٌ مَعَ صَدِيقٍ لِى.
Are you (all) from Delhi?	hal 'aan töm min dil hî?	هَلُ أنتُم مِنْ دلهى؟
Yes, we are from Delhi.	na a'am, naH nö min dil hî.	نَعَمُ، نَحُنُ مِن دلهى.
No, we are from Mumbai.	lã naH nö min möm bãî.	لَا، نَحُنُ مِنْ مومباى.
Are you hungry.	hal 'aan ta jaw a'ãn?	هَلُ أنتَ جَوعَان؟
Yes,	na a'am,	نَعَمُ،
I am hungry.	'aa nã jaw a'ãn.	أنَاجَوعَان.

64

English	Transliteration	Arabic
Are you thirsty?	hal 'aan ta a'a† Šãn?	هَل أنتَ عطشان؟
Yes,	na a'am,	نَعَم ،
I am thirsty.	'aa nã a'a† Šãn.	أنَا عَطْشَان .
Any service/Can I do something for you?	'aay yö Kid ma?	أىُّ خِدْمَةٍ ؟
No, thanks.	lã, Šök ran	لَا شُكراً .
Is Mr. Jameel in ?/	ha lis say yid	هل السيد
Is Mr. Jameel	ja mîl	جَميل
available?	maw jðd?	مَوجُود؟
Yes,	na a'am ,	نَعَم ،
he is in	hö wa maw jðd.	هُو مَوجُود .
What do you want?	mã Ðã tö rîd ?	مَاذَاتريدُ ؟
I want to	'aö rîd	اريدُ
see him .	mö qã ba la ta hö.	مُقَابَلَتَه .
What is your name?	mas mök?	مَاسْمُك ؟
My name is Shanker.	'ais mî Šan kar.	اسمى شنكر .
I have come on	ji'a tö fî	جِئتُ فى
a special	mö him ma tin	مُهِمَّةٍ
mission.	Kã S Sa tin.	خَاصَّةٍ .
Please come, this way.	ta fad dal min hö nã.	تَفَضَّلُ مِن هُنَا .
Mr. Jameel	as say yid ja mîl	السَيِّد جميل
is waiting for you.	fîn ti zã rik.	فى انتظارك .

Exercise		التمرين
Question (1)		السؤال (١)
Where from	min 'aay na	من أين
is Ram Kumar?	rãm kð mãr?	رام كومار؟
Answer		الجواب
Ram Kumar	rãm kð mãr	رام كومار
is from	min wi lã yat	من ولاية
Bihar state	bî hãr.	بيهار.
Question (2)		السؤال (٢)
Are you (p.m)	hal 'aan töm	هل أنتم
from Varanasi?	min fã rã na sî.	من فارانسي
Answer		الجواب
No, we are	lã, naH nö	لا، نحن
from Kerala	min ki rã lã.	من كيرالا.
Question (3)		السؤال (٣)
Is she	hal hi ya	هل هى
thirsty	a'a† Šã na	عطشانة
and hungry?	wa jaw a'ã na?	و جوعانة؟
Yes, she is	na a'am, hi ya	نعم، هى
thirsty	a'a† Šã na	عطشانة

66

English	Transliteration	Arabic
and hungry	wa jaw a'ã na.	و جوعانة.
Question (4)		السؤال(٤)
Is Mohammad	hal mö *Ham* mad	هل محمد
tired?	taa' bãn?	تعبان؟
Answer		الجواب
Yes, Mohammad	na a'am mö *Ham* mad	نعم، محمد
is tired.	taa' bãn?	تعبان.
Question (5)		السؤال(٥)
Is Mr.	ha lis say yid	هل السيد
Menon	mî nõn	مينون
in/available?	maw jõd?	موجود؟
Answer		الجواب
No, he	lã, hö wa	لا، هو
has left.	K ra ja.	خرج.

❁☆☆☆❁

Lesson 11

Conversation

محادثة

English	Transliteration	Arabic
Visitor:	az zã 'air:	<div dir="rtl">اَلزَّائِر:</div>
Good morning,	Sa bã Hal Kayr	<div dir="rtl">صَبَاحَ الخَير</div>
sir.	yã say yi dî.	<div dir="rtl">يَاسَيِّدِى.</div>
Office employee:	mö waz za föl mak tab:	<div dir="rtl">مُوَظَّفُ المَكتَب:</div>
Good morning.	Sa bã Han nðr.	<div dir="rtl">صَبَاحَ النُّور.</div>
How do you do?	kay fal Hãl?	<div dir="rtl">كَيْفَ الحَال؟</div>
Visitor:	az zã 'air:	<div dir="rtl">اَلزَّائِر:</div>
Good.	†ay yib.	<div dir="rtl">طَيِّبٌ.</div>
And how do you do?	wa kay fan ta?	<div dir="rtl">وَكَيْفَ أَنتَ؟</div>
Office employee:	mö waz za föl mak tab:	<div dir="rtl">مُوَظَّفُ المَكتَب:</div>
I am good.	'aa nã bi Kayr.	<div dir="rtl">أَنَابخَير.</div>
All praise to Allah.	al Ham dö lil lãh.	<div dir="rtl">الحَمدُلِلَّه.</div>
And who are you?	wa man 'aan ta?	<div dir="rtl">وَمَنْ أَنتَ؟</div>
Visitor:	az zã 'air :	<div dir="rtl">اَلزَّائِر:</div>
I am the representative	'aa nã mö maT Til	<div dir="rtl">أَنَا مُمَثِّل</div>
of. E.P. I.	Ša ri kat E.P.I.	<div dir="rtl">شِرِكَة اى، بى، ئى.</div>
Office employee:	mö waz za föl maktab:	<div dir="rtl">مُوَظَّفُ المَكتَب:</div>
What is your name?	mas mök?	<div dir="rtl">مَااسمُك؟</div>

68

Visitor :	az zã 'air:	اَلزَّائِر:
My name is Ahmad .	'ais mî 'aa*H* mad .	اسمى احمد .
Office employee:	mö waz za föl mak tab:	مُوَظَّفُ الْمَكْتَب:
What do you want?	mã Đã tö rîd?	مَاذَا تُرِيدُ؟
I want to meet/see	'aö rîd 'aö qã bil	أَرِيدُ أَقَابِل
the office head /	ra 'aî sal mak tab/	رَئِيسَ الْمَكْتَب /
the office director,	mö dîr al mak tab:	مُدِيرَالْمَكْتَب،
please.	min fa*d* lik.	مِنْ فَضْلِك .
Give	hãt kãrt	هَاتِ كَارت
your card.	*H*ad ra tik.	حَضرَتِك .
Please/here it is.	ta fa*d* *d*al.	تَفَضَّلُ .
Sit down	'aij lis,	إِجْلِس ،
and wait for a while.	wan ta zir qa lî lan.	وَانْتَظِر قَلِيلاً .
Visitor:	'aaz zã 'air:	اَلزَّائِر:
sorry,	'aã sif,	آسِف ،
I am busy .	'aa nã maŠ ghöl.	أَنَا مَشْغُول .
Fix my appointment	*H*ad did maw a'i dî	حَدِّدْ مَوعِدِى
with him tomorrow.	ma a'a hö gha dan.	مَعَه غَداً.
Take	hãk	هَاك
telephon No.	raq mat ti li fön.	رَقم التلفون.

69

Inform me	'aaK bir nî	أَخْبِرنِي
about the appointment	bil maw a'i di	بِالمَوعِد
on the telephone.	a'a lat ti li fõn.	عَلىٰ التلفون .
After	wa baa' das sã a'a til	وَبَعدَ السَّاعةِ
5.P.M.,	Kã mi sa ma sã 'aan	الخَامِسَة مَسَاءً
I will wait	'aa kð nö fin ti zãr	أَكُونُ فِى انتِظَارِ
for your call .	ti li fõ nik.	تلفونك .
Office employee:	mö waz za föl mak tab:	مُوَظَّفُ المَكتَب:
Good.	†ay yib.	طَيِّب .
God willing,	'ain Šã 'aal lãh,	إن شَاءَ اللَّه ،
I will inform you in the	'aöK bi rök	أَخْبِرك
evening.	bil ma sã 'ai.	بِالمَسَاءِ.

Exercise التمرين

Question (1)		السؤال (١)
How did the visitor	kay fa ba da 'a	كَيفَ بَدأ
begin to talk?	az zã 'ai röl Ha dîT?	الزَّائِرُ الحَدِيث ؟
Answer		الجواب
The visitor began to talk	ba da 'aaz zã 'ai rö l-Ha	بَدأ الزَّائِر
with greeting	dî Ta bit ta Hîya .	الحَدِيث بِالتَّحِيَّة .

70

English	Transliteration	Arabic
He said:	qã la:	قَالَ :
Good morning	_Sa bã _Hal _Kayr.	صَبَاحَ الْخَيرِ .
Question (2)		السؤال (٢)
What did	mã Ðã qã la	مَاذَ اقَالَ
the employee	mö waz za föl	مُوَظّفُ الْمَكْتَب؟
say?	mak tab?	
Answer		الجواب
The empolyee	mö waz za föl mak tab	مُوَظّفُ الْمَكْتَب
returned the greeting.	rad da bit taHï ya.	رَدَّ بِالتَّحِيِّةِ .
He said:	qã la:	قَالَ :
Good morning /	_Sa bã _Han nðr.	صَبَاحَ النُّورِ.
morning of light.		
Question (3)		السؤال (٣)
What did the office	mã Ðã sa 'aa la	مَاذَ اسَأَلَ
employee ask	mö waz za föl mak ta	مُوَظّفُ الْمَكْتَب
the visitor?	biz zã 'air?	اَلزَّائِرِ؟
Answer		الجواب
The office empolyee	sa 'aa la mö waz zaf öl	سَأَلَ مُوَظّفُ
asked the visitor:	mak ta biz zã 'air:	الْمَكْتَب اَلزَّائِرَ:
Who are you?	man 'aan ta?	مَنْ أنتِ؟

Question (4)		السؤال (٤)
What did	mã Ðã qã laz	مَا ذَاقَالَ
the visitor say?	zã 'air?	الزَّائِر؟
Answer		الجواب
The visitor said:	qã laz zã 'air:	قَالَ الزَّائِر:
I am the representative	'aa nã mö maⱢⱢil	أَنَامُمَثِّلُ
of E.P.I.	Ša ri kat	شَرِكَة
company.	E.P.I.	اى ، بى ، ئى.
I want to meet/see	'aö rîd 'aö qã bil	أَرِيدُ أَقَابِل
office head.	ra 'aî sal mak tab.	رَئِيسَ الْمَكْتَب .
Question (5)		السؤال(٥)
What did the office	mã Ðã qã la mö wa<u>z</u>	مَاذَا قَالَ مُوَظَّفُ
employee say?	<u>z</u>a föl mak tab?	الْمَكْتَب؟
Answer:		الجواب
The office employee	qã la mö wa<u>z</u> <u>z</u>a föl	قَالَ مُوَظَّفُ
said:	mak tab:	الْمَكْتَب:
Please, Come.	ta fa*d dal*.	تَفَضَّلُ .
Sit down,	'aij lis.	إِجْلِس .
And wait for a while.	wan ta <u>z</u>ir qa lî lan.	وَانْتَظِرْقَلِيلًا .
Question(6)		السؤال (٦)
What did the	mã Ðã	مَاذَا
visitor say?	qã laz zã 'air?	قَالَ الزَّائِر؟

English	Transliteration	Arabic
Answer		الجواب
The visitor said:	qã laz zã 'air:	قَالَ الزَّائِر:
Please,	min fad lik.	مِنْ فَضْلِك .
fix my appointment	Had did maw a'i dî	حَدِّد مَوعِدِى
with him tomorrow.	ma a'a hö gha dan.	مَعَه غداً.
Take /note	hãk	هَاك
telephone no.	raq mat ti li fõn.	رَقم التلفون
Inform me about	'aaK bir nî	أخُبِرنِى
appointment	bil maw a'id	بالمَوعِد
on this telephone	a'a lã hã Ðat ti li fõn	علىٰ هذا التلفون
in the evening.	bil ma sã 'ai.	بالمَسَاء .
I'll be waiting	'aa kõn fin ti zãr.	أكُونُ فى انتظار .
Question (7)		السؤال (٧)
What did the office	mã Ðã qã la mö waz	مَاذَاقَالَ مُوَظَّفُ
employee say?	za fõl mak tab?	المَكتَب؟
Answer		الجواب
Good.	†ay yib	طَيِّب .
God so willing,	'ain Ša 'aal lãh,	إن شَاءَ الله ،
I will inform you	'aöK bi rö köm	أخُبِركُم
in the evening	bil ma sã 'ai	بالمَسَاء
about the appointment.	bil maw a'id.	بالمَوعِد.

◈☆☆☆☆◈

Lesson 12

محادثة بالمطعم

Coversation at the restaurant

Customer:	az za bǒn.	<div dir="rtl">اَلزَّبُون :</div>
Garcon /waiter	ghãr sǒn .	<div dir="rtl">غَارسُون .</div>
Yes sir/ in your attendance.	Hã dir yã say yi dî.	<div dir="rtl">حَاضِر يَاسَيِّدى .</div>

Customer :	az za bǒn:	<div dir="rtl">اَلزَّبُون:</div>
Where is the menu?	'aay nal qã 'ai ma?	<div dir="rtl">أينَ القَائِمَة ؟</div>
Garcon :	ghãr sǒn:	<div dir="rtl">غَارسُون :</div>
Here it is sir.	hãk yã say yi dî.	<div dir="rtl">هَاك يَاسَيِّدى .</div>
Customer:	az za bǒn:	<div dir="rtl">اَلزَّبُون:</div>
Bring cold water.	hãt al mã 'aal bã rid.	<div dir="rtl">هَاتِ المَاءَ البَارِدَ.</div>
Garcon :	ghãr sǒn:	<div dir="rtl">غَارسُون :</div>
At your service, sir.	Hã dir yã say yi dî.	<div dir="rtl">حَاضِر يَاسَيِّدى .</div>

Customer:	az za bǒn:	<div dir="rtl">اَلزَّبُون:</div>
Good, bring now	†ay yib, hãt al ãa na	<div dir="rtl">طَيِّب ، هَاتِ الآنَ</div>
one bread	a'ay Šan wã Hi dan	<div dir="rtl">عيشاً واحدا</div>
and one plate of	wa †a ba qan min al	<div dir="rtl">وطَبقاً مِن</div>

English	Transliteration	Arabic
rice and	'aö röz wa	الْأُرُزَّ وَ
vegetable soup/	Šör ba Köd rã wãt/	شُوربة خُضْراوَات/
bone soup/	Šör bã a'i zãm/	شُوربة عِظَام /
tomato soup	Šör bã ṭa mã ṭim	شُوربة طَمَاطِم /
and mutton	wa laH man	وَلَحُماً
curry	ṭa bî Kan	طَبِيخاً
and half a plate of mniced	wa niSf ṭa baq	ونصف طبق
meat.	mi nal laH mil	مِنَ اللَّحِم
Garcon:	maf rðm.	المَفرُوم .
At your service sir /	ghãr sðn:	غَارسُون :
yes sir.	Hã dir yã say yi dî.	حَاضِر يَا سَيِّدى .
Any other thing.	'aay yö Hã ja 'aöK rã?	أَىُّ حَاجَةٍ أخرى؟
Customer:	az za bðn:	الزَّبُون:
Yes, I want	na a'am, 'aö rîd	نَعَم ، أُرِيدُ
also	'aay dan	أيضاً
fried chicken	da jã jan maq lî yan	دَجَاجاً مَقْلِيًّا
and ice cream .	wa bð zã / 'aays krîm.	وَبُوظَة / أيس كريم،
Garcon:	ghãr sðn:	غَارسُون :
O.K. sir.	Hã dir yã say yi dî.	حَاضِر يَا سَيِّدى .
Do you want tea	'aa tö rîd Ša yan	أتُرِيد شَاياً

75

English	Transliteration	Arabic
or coffee?	'aam qah wa?	أَمْ قَهوة ؟
Customer:	az za bǒn:	اَلزَّبُون:
I don,t want tea.	lã 'aö rîd Šã yan.	لاَ أُرِيدُ شاياً .
I want coffee	'aö rîd qah wã	أُرِيدُ قَهوة
with milk/	ma a'al Ha lîb/	مَعَ الحَليب /
I want coffee	'aö rîd qah wã	أُرِيدُ قَهوة
without milk.	bi dǒ nil Ha lîb.	بِدُونِ الحَليب .
I request you/	wa 'aar jǒk	وَأرجُوك
please pack for me some	'aan ta löf fa lî	أَنْ تَلُفَّ لِى
sandwiches	send wî Šat	سند ويشات
of cheese	jöb nã	مِنْ جُبنَة
and butter.	wa zöb da.	وَزُبدَة .
I also want	ka Ðã lik 'aö rîd	كَذلِك أُرِيدُ
some	baa' dan mi nal	بَعضاً مِنَ
boiled eggs.	bay dil mas lǒq.	البَيضِ المَسلُوقِ .
Garcon:	ghãr sǒn:	غَارسُون :
At your service, sir.	Hã dir ya say yi dî.	حَاضِر يَاسَيِّدى .
Customer: Waiter.	'aaz za bǒn: ghãr sǒn.	اَلزَّبُون: غَارسُون .
Waiter:	ghãr sǒn:	غَارسُون :
Yes, sir.	na a'am, yã say yi dî.	نَعَم ، يَاسَيِّدى .

Customer:	az za bŏn:	اَلزَّبُون:
Bring now	hã til'aã na	هَاتِ الآن
the bill.	al fã tŏ ra .	الفَاتُورَة .
Waiter:	ghãr sŏn:	غَارسُون :
At your service, sir!	*Hã dir* yã say yi dî.	حَاضِر يَاسَيِّدِى .

Execise
التمرين

Question (1)
السُؤال (١)

Whom does the	ma nil la Ðî	مَن الَّذِى
customer call?	yŏ nã dîhiz za bŏn?	يُنَادِيه الزَّبون؟

Answer
الجواب

The customer calls the	'aaz za bŏn yŏ nã dî	اَلزَّبُون يُنَادِى
garcon/waiter.	al ghãr sŏn.	الغَارسُون .

Question (2)
السؤال (٢)

What does	mã Ðã ya qŏ löz	مَاذَايَقُولُ
the customer ask?	za bŏn?	اَلزَّبُون؟

Answer
الجواب

The customer asks	ya† löb az za bŏn	يَطلُبُ الزَّبُون
for the menu.	al qã 'ai ma	القَائِمة
	bi† †a a'ãm	بالطَّعَام .

77

Question (3)		السؤال (٣)
What does the	mã Đã ya†löb	مَاذَا يَطْلُبُ
customer ask?	az za bŏn?	الزَّبُونُ ؟
Answer		الجواب
The customer asks (for)	ya† löb 'aaz za bŏn	يَطْلُبُ الزَّبُون
cold water	al mã 'aal bã rid	اَلْمَاءَ البَارِد
and also	wa ka Đã liḳ	وَكَذلك
asks for	ya† löb ka Tîran min	يَطْلُبُ
a lot of food.	al 'aa† a'i ma.	كَثِيراً مِنَ الأَطْعِمَة.
Question (4)		السؤال (٤)
Does the customer ask for	'aa ya† lö böz za bŏn	أَيَطْلُبُ الزبون
the fried chicken	da jã jan maq lî yan	دَجَاجاً مقَلِيًّا
or roast chicken?	'aw da jã jan maŠ wî yan	أودَجَاجاًمَشْوِياً ؟
Answer		الجواب
The customer asks	ya† lö böz za bŏn	يطلُبُ الزَّبُون
for fried chicken.	da jã jan maq lî yan	دَجَاجاً مَقْلِياً.
Question (5)		السؤال (٥)
What does the	mã Đã yas 'aa lö hö	مَاذَا يَسْأَلُه
garcon ask him?	al ghãr sŏn?	الغَارسُون؟

English	Transliteration	Arabic
Answer		الجواب
The garcon asks :	yas 'aa löhö al ghãr	يَسْأَلُه الغَارِسُون:
Do you want tea	sðn:	أَتُرِيدُ شَاياً
or coffee?	'aa tö rîd Šã yan	أَمْ قَهْوَةً ؟
Question (6)	'aam qah wã?	السؤال (٦)
What does the customer		مَاذَا يَقُولُ
say?	mã Ðã ya qð löz	الزَّبون ؟
Answer	za bðn?	الجواب
The customer says:	ya qð löz za bðn:	يَقُولُ الزَّبون :
I don't want tea.	lã 'aö rîd Šã yan.	لَا أُرِيدُ شَاياً .
I want coffee	'aö rîd qah wã	أُرِيدُ قَهوة
with milk	ma a'al Ha lîb	مَعَ الحَلِيب
and also	wa ka Ðã lik	وَكَذلِك
the customer asks for	ya† löböz za bðn	يَطْلُبُ
the bill.	al fã tð rã.	الزَّبُونَ أَلفَاتُورَة .

◈☆☆☆◈

79

Lesson 13

محادثة بِالمَحل / الدكان
Conversation at the shop

English	Transliteration	Arabic
A customer enters	yad Köl za bŏn	يَدخُل زَبُون
a shop.	dök kã nan.	دُكَّانا.
The shopowner	yö raH Hib bi hi	يُرَحَّبُ بِه
welcomes him	Sã Hi böl ma Hal li	صَاحِبُ المَحَلِّ
and they (both) have	wa yaj rî bay na hö mã	وَيَجْرى بَينَهُمَا
the following conversation.	al Ha dî Tat tã lî.	اَلحَدِيثُ التَّالى .
Shopowner:	Sã Hi böl ma Hal li:	صَاحِبُ المَحَلِّ :
Good day,	†ãb yaw mök,	طَابَ يَومُكَ،
sir.	yã say yi dî.	يَاسَيِّدى
Can I help you?	'aay yö Kid ma?	أَىُّ خِدمَةٍ ؟
Customer:	az za bŏn:	الزبون:
Good day.	†ãb yaw mök.	طَابَ يَومُك .
I want a shirt.	'aö rîd qa mî San.	أَريدُ قَميصاً.
Shopowner:	Sã Hi böl ma Hal li:	صَاحِبُ المَحَلِّ :
Which colour?	'aay yö lawn?	أَىُّ لَونٍ ؟
red	'aaH mar	أَحمَر
blue	'aaz raq	أزرَق

80

black	'aas wad	أَسْوَد
white	'aab ya*d*	أَبيَض
sky blue	'aaz raq sa mã wî.	أَرْزق سَمَاوى.
Customer:	az za bŏn:	الزَّبُون :
I want	'aö rîd	أُريدُ
a white shirt.	qa mî *S*an 'aab ya*d*.	قَميصاً أَبيَض .
Shopowner:	*S*ã *H*i böl ma *H*al li:	صَاحبُ المَحَلِّ :
At your service, sir.	*H*ã *d*ir yã say yi dî.	حَاضِر يَاسَيِّدى.
What is your size?	kam ma qã sök?	كَمُ مَقَاسُك؟
Customer:	az za bŏn :	الزَّبُون :
It is forty	hö wa 'aar ba a'ð na	هُوَ اربَعُون
centimetres.	sin tî mî tar.	سينتيميتر.
And I want	wa 'aö rîd	وَأُريدُ
the best quality.	'aaf *d*a la nawa'.	أَفضَل نَوع .
Shopowner:	*S*ã *H*i böl ma *H*al li:	صَاحبُ المَحَلِّ :
Your order is	'aam rök	أَمرُك
obeyed/ you are obeyed.	mö †ãa' .	مُطَاعٌ .
Here is the one you are	hãk	هَاك
looking for,	man Šŏ dak	مَنْشُودك
sir.	yã say yi dî.	يَاسَيِّدى.

Customer:	az za bŏn:	الزَّبُون :
This is beautiful/this is good.	hã Ðã ja mîl.	هَذاجَمِيلٌ .
What is its price?	kam Ta ma nŏh?	كَمْ ثَمَنُه ؟
Shopkeeper:	Sã Hi bŏl ma Hal li?	صَاحِبُ المَحَلّ ؟
It is thirty	hŏ wa Ta lã Tŏ na	هُو ثَلاثُون
pounds.	jŏ nay han.	جُنَيهاً .
Customer:	az za bŏn:	الزَّبُون :
Agreed/o.k.	mŏ wã fiq.	مُوافِق .
Pack it, please.	lŏf fa hŏ min fad lik.	لُفَّه مِنْ فَضْلِك .
Shopkeeper:	Sã Hi bŏl ma Hal li:	صَاحِبُ المَحَلّ :
At your service,	taH tam rik	تَحْتَ أمرِك
sir.	yã say yi dî .	يَاسَيِّدى .
Do you want	hal tŏ rîd	هَلُ تُرِيدُ
any other thing	si yã da tŏk Šay 'aan	سِيَادَتُك شَيئاً
Sir?	'aã Kar?	آخَر؟
Customer:	az za bŏn:	اَلزَّبُون:
Not now.	lay sal 'aã na.	لَيسَ الآن .
Some other time,	fî waq tin 'aã Kar	فِى وَقتٍ آخَر،
God so willing.	'ain Šã 'aal lã hŏ.	إِن شَاءَ اللَّه .

Shopkeeper:	_S_ã _H_i böl ma _H_al li :	صَاحِبُ المَحَلِّ :
You will always	saw fa ta ji dö nã	سَوفَ تَجِدُنَا
find us at	dã 'ai man fî	دَائِماً فِى
your service,	_K_id ma tik,	خِدمَتِك،
God so willing.	'ain Ša 'aal lãh.	إن شَاءَ اللَّه.
Customer:	az za bön:	اَلزَّبُون :
Can you	hal yom kin lak	هَلُ يُمُكِن لَك
tell me	ta qöl lî	تَقُولُ لِى
how to go	kay fa 'aam Šî	كَيفَ أمشِى
to post office?	'ai lã mak ta bil ba rîd?	إلى مَكتَبِ البَرِيد؟
Shopkeeper:	_S_ã _H_i böl ma _H_al li:	صَاحِبُ المَحَلِّ :
The post office	mak ta bol ba rîd	مَكتَبُ البَرِيد
is far away from here,	ba a'îd min hö na ,	بَعيدٌ مِن هُنا،
you can take	möm kin ta'a _K_öÐ	مُمكِن تَاخُذ
bus	'að tð bîs	أُوتوبيس
or taxi.	'aaw tãk sî.	اوتاكسى.
Customer:	az za bön:	الزَّبُون :
Where is the	'aay na maw qi föl	أينَ مَوقِفُ
bus stop/	al 'að tð bîs /	الاوتوبيس/
the taxi stand.	maw qi föt tãk sî?	مَوقِفُ التاكسى ؟

83

Shopkeeper:	_Sā Hi böl ma Hal li:	صَاحِبُ المَحَلِّ :
You have to walk	tam Ši	تَمشِى
a little. you will find the	qa lî lan. ta ji döl	قَلِيلاً . تَجِدُ
stand	maw qif	المَوقِف
on your right hand/	a'a lã ya mî nik/	على يَمِينِك /
on your left hand.	a'a lã ya sã rik .	على يَسَارِك .
Take No	_Köð raqm	خُذ رَقم
40.	'aar ba a'ðn.	أربعون .
This bus will reach	yð _Si lök hã Ðal	يُوصِلُك هذا
you the	'að tð ط؟ 'ai lã	الاوتوبيس الى
post office.	mak ta bil ba rîd.	مَكتَبِ البَرِيد .
Customer:	az za bðn:	اَلزَّبُون :
Thanks o'brother	Šök ran ya 'aa _Kî.	شُكراً يَا أخى .
Shopkeeper:	_Sā Hi böl ma Hal li:	صَاحِبُ المَحَلِّ :
Mention not,	a'af wan	عَفُواً
sir.	yã say yi dî.	يَاسَيِّدِى .

Exercise		التمرين
Question (1)		السؤال (١)
Who enters	man yad _Köl	مَن يَّدخُلُ
the shop?	al ma Hal la/addökkãn	المَحَلَّ / الدُّكَان ؟

84

Answer		الجواب
A customer enters	yad <u>K</u>ö lö za bǒn	يَدخُلُ زَبُون
the shop.	ad dök kãn.	الدُّكَان
Qusetion (2)		السؤال (٢)
What does the	mã Đã ya qǒ lö	مَاذَايَقُولُ
shopkeeper say?	<u>S</u>ã <i>H</i>i böl ma <i>H</i>al li?	صَاحِبُ المَحَلِّ ؟
Answer		الجواب
The sohpkeeper	yö ra<i>H</i> <i>H</i>i bö bi hi	يُرَحِّبُ بِه
welcomes him	<u>S</u>ã <i>H</i>i böl ma <i>H</i>al li	صَاحِبُ المَحَلِّ
saying:	qã 'ai lan:	قَائِلًا :
Good day,	†ãb yaw mök	طَابَ يَومُك
sir.	yã say yi dî.	يَاسَيِّدِى .
Question (3)		السؤال (٣)
What does the	mã Đã ya qǒ löz	مَاذَا يَقُولُ
customer say?	za bǒn?	الزَّبُون ؟
Answer		الجواب
The customer	az za bǒn	اَلزَّبُون
returns the greetings.	ya röd döt ta <i>H</i>î ya.	يَرُدُّ التَّحِيَّة .
Question (4)		السؤال(٤)
What does the	mã Đã ya† lö böz	مَاذَايَطلُبُ

customer ask?	za bðn?	الزَّبُون ؟
Answer		الجواب
The customer asks for a	ya† lö böz za bðn	يَطْلُبُ الزَّبُون
white shirt.	qa mî _S_an 'aab ya_d_.	قَمِيصاًأبيض .
Question (5)		السؤال (٥)
How much	kam _T_a ma nöl	كَمُ ثَمنُ
is the shirt?	qa mî_S_ ?	القَميص؟
Answer		الجواب
It is 30	ho wa _T_a lã _Tð_ na	هُو ثَلاثُون
pounds	jö nay han.	جُنَيهاً .
Question (6)		السؤال (٦)
Does the customer buy	hal ya_Š_ ta riz za bðn	هَلُ يَشتَرِى الزبون
any other thing?	_Š_ay 'aan 'aã _K_a ra?	شَيئاً آخر؟
Answer		الجواب
No, customer does not	lã, lã ya_Š_ ta riz	لا، لايَشتَرِى
buy	za bðn	الزَّبُون
any other thing.	_Š_ay 'aan 'aã _K_a ra.	شَيئاً آخر.
Question (7)		السؤال (٧)
What does the	mã Ðã yas aa löz	مَاذَا يَسألُ

86

English	Transliteration	Arabic
customer ask	za bðn	الزَّبون
the shopkeeper	Sã Hi bal ma Hal li	صَاحِب المَحَلَّ
after buying	baa' da Ši rã 'ail	بَعدَ شِرَاءِ
the shirt?	qa miS?	القَميص ؟
Answer		الجواب
The customer asks him	yas 'aa lö höz za bðn	يَسألُه الزَّبُون
about the address	a'an a'ön wãn	عن غُنوان
of the post office.	mak ta bil ba rîd .	مَكتَبِ البَريد .
Question (8)		السؤال(٨)
What does	mã Ðã ya qð lö lahö	مَاذَا يَقولُ لَه
the shopkeeper tell him?	Sã Hi böl ma Hal li?	صَاحِبُ المَحَلَّ ؟
Answer		الجواب
The shopkeeper	ya qð lö la hö	يَقُولُ له
tells him:	Sã Hi böl ma Hal li:	صَاحِبُ المَحَلَّ :
This place is far away,	hã Ðal ma kã nö baa'îd	هذاالمَكَانُ بَعيدٌ
sir.	yã say yi dî.	يَاسَيِّدى .
You may take	möm kin ta'a KoÐ	مُمُكِن تَاخُذ
bus	'að tð bis	اوتوبيس
or taxi.	'aaw tãk sî.	أوتاكسى .

87

Question (9)		السؤال (٩)
What does the	mã Ðã ya qð lö la höz	مَاذَا يَقُولُ له
customer say?	za bðn?	الزَّبون ؟
Answer		الجواب
The customer thanks him	yaŠ kö rö höz za bðn	يَشكُرُه الزَّبُون
saying:	qã 'ai lan:	قَائِلاً :
Thanks brother.	Šök ran yã 'aa Kî	شُكرأَيَاأَخِى
Question (10)		السؤال (١٠)
How does	kay fa ya röd dö	كَيفَ يَرُدُّ
the shopkeeper	a'a lay hi	عليه
reply?	<u>S</u>ã <u>H</u>i böl ma <u>H</u>al li?	صَاحِبُ المَحَلِّ؟
Answer		الجواب
The shopkeeper	ya qð lö la hð	يَقُولُ لَه
replies	<u>S</u>ã <u>H</u>i böl ma <u>H</u>al li	صَاحِبُ المَحَلِّ
respectfully:	bi 'aa dab:	بِأَدبٍ:
Mentoin not	a'af wan	عَفوأ
sir.	yã say yi di.	يَاسَيِّدِى

◆☆☆☆◆

Lesson 14

محادثة عن تبديل العملة

Conversation about changing currency

A foreigner customer	za bŏn 'aaj na bî	زبون أَجْنَبِي
at a hotel	bi fŏn döq	بفندق
speaks	ya ta Had da Tö	يتحدَّث
to a clerk	'ai lã kã tib	إلى كَاتِب
and they	wa yaj rî	و يَجْرِي
have the	bay na hö mã	بَيْنَهُمَا
following converstion:	al Ha dîT at tã lî:	الحَدِيث التَّالِي:
The foreigner customer:	az za bŏn al 'aaj na bî:	الزَّبُون الأَجْنَبِي:
sir?	say ya dî?	سيِّدي؟
The clerk:	al kã tib:	الكَاتب:
yes sir,	na a'am yã say yi dî,	نعم ياسيِّدي،
Customer:	az za bŏn:	الزَّبون:
I want to	'aö rîd	أُرِيد
change the currency	tab dî lal a'öm la.	تَبْدِيلَ العُمْلَة.
Where is it	'aay na yöm kin	أَيْنَ يُمْكِن
possible?	Đã lik?	ذَلِكَ؟
The clerk:	al kã tib:	الكَأتِب:

English	Transliteration	Arabic
We have this	la day nã hã Đi his	لَدينا هَذِه
facility	sö hð la	السُّهُولة
in this hotel,	fî hã Đal fön döq,	فى هذَا الفُنْدُق،
sir.	yã say yi dî,	يَا سَيِّدى.
Which currency	'aay yö a'öm la tin	أى عُملةٍ
do you have?	a'in dak?	عِندَك؟
The customer:	az za bðn:	الزّبون:
I have	a'ni dî	عِنْدِي
American dollar.	dð lãr 'aam rî kî.	دُوْلَار أُمرِيْكي.
The clerk:	al kã tib:	الكَاتِب:
Sorry sir.	'aã sif yã say yi dî.	آسِف يا سَيِّدى.
We don't have	ma a'in da nã	ماَ عِندنا
today's rate	sia' röl yawm	سِعرالْيَوَم
for American	lid dð lãr	لِلدُّوْلار
dollar.	al 'aam rî kî.	الأُمرِيْكي.
You may go	möm kin taĐ hab	مُمْكِن تَذهَب
to the central	'ai lal bank	إلى البَنك
Bank	al mar ka zî	المَركَزِى
to change	li tab dîl	لَتبِديل
your dollars.	dð lã rã tik.	دُوْلارَاتِك.

90

The customer:	az za bŏn:	الزَّبُون:
Thank you	Šök ran	شُكُرا
brother.	yã 'aa Kî.	يا أخِي.
Where is	'aay nal	أينَ
the central Bank?	ban kal mar ka zî?	الْبنك المركزي؟
The clerk:	al kã tib:	الكاتِب:
It is	hö wa	هُوَ
near.	qa rîb.	قَرِيب.
You may walk	möm kin tam Šî	مُمكِن تَمشِى
on foot.	a'a lal 'aaq dãm	على الاقدَام.
Five minutes	Kam sa da qã 'aiq	خَمسَ دَقَائِق
only from here.	fa qa† min hö nã.	فَقط مِن هُنَا.
You"ll find	ta ji döl	تَجِدُ
the Central Bank	ban kal mar ka zî	البَنك المَركَزِى
at the end	bi ni hã yat	بِنِهاية
of this street/road.	hã ĐãŠ Šã ria'.	هذا الشَّارِع.
The customer leaves	yaK rö jöz za bŏn	يَخرُجُ الزبون
and walks to the Central	wa yam Šî 'ai lal	وَ يَمشِى الى
Bank.	ban kil mar ka zî.	البَنكِ المَركَزِى.
The customer enters the	yad Kö löz za bŏn	يَدخُلُ الزَّبُونُ

91

English	Transliteration	Arabic
Central Bank	al ban kal mar ka zî	البَنك المَركَزى
and he goes	wa yaÐ ha bö	وَ يَذهَبُ
to the counter	'ai lã Šöb bãk	إلى شُبّاك
of currency exchange (exchange counter).	tab dî lîl a'öm lãt.	تَبديلِ العُملَات.
The foreigner customer (says)	az za bð nöl 'aaj na bî	الزَّبُون الأجنَبى
to the cashier:	li 'aa mîni_S_ _S_ön ðöq:	لِأمينِ الصُّندوق:
I want	'aö rîd	أريدُ
to change currency.	tab dî lal a'öm la.	تَبديل العُملة.
Cashier:	'aa mî nö_S_ _S_ön ðöq:	أمينُ الصُّندوق:
Well, sir.	†ay yib yã say yi dî.	طَيِّب، يَا سَيِّدى.
What do you have?	mã Ðã a'in dak?	مَاذَا عِندك؟
Customer:	az za bðn:	الزبون:
I have dollars	a'in dî dð lã rãt.	عِندى دولارات.
How much is $?	kam sia' röd dð lãr?	كَمْ سِعر الدولار؟
Cashier:	'aa mî nö_S_ _S_ön ðöq:	أمينُ الصندوق:
We take dollar	na'a _K_öÐ 'aad dð lãr	نَأخُذُ الدولار
for forty	bi 'aar ba a'î na	بِأربعين
rupees.	rð bî ya.	روبية.

English	Transliteration	Arabic
It is today's rate.	hö wa sia' röl yawm.	هو سِعرُ اليَوم.
It is the offical	wa hö was sia' rör	وَ هو السِّعر
rate .	ras mî.	الرَّسمى.
Customer:	az za bðn:	الزبون:
Good, I want	†ay yib , 'aö rîd	طَيِّب، أريد
to change one hundred	tab dîl mi 'aat	تَبْديلُ مِئة
dollars.	dð lãr .	دولار.
Cashier:	'aa mî nöS Sön dðq:	أمينُ الصُّندوق:
Yes , sir	Hã dir yã say yi dî.	حاضِر، سيدى-
Cashier	'aa mî nöS Sön dðq	أمينُ الصُّندوق
takes the	ya'a Kö Ðö	يَأخُذُ
dollars	'aad dð lã rãt	الدولارات
and counts them.	wa ya a'öd dö hã.	ويَعُدَّها.
Then he counts	Töm ma ya a'öd dö	ثُمَّ يَعُدُّ
the rupees	ar rð bi yãt	الروبيات
and gives it over	wa yö sal li mö hã	وَيُسَلِّمُها
to the foriegner customer.	liz za bð nil aj na bî.	للزبون الاجنبى .
The foreigner customer	az za bð nöl 'aaj na bî	الزبون الاجنبى
receives the rupees	yas ta li mö ar rð bîyãt	يَسْتَلم الروبيات
and he counts it .	wa ya a'öd dö hã.	وَيَعُدُّها .

93

Then he puts it	Töm ma ya da a'ö hã	ثُمَّ يَضَعُهَا
in his purse.	fî kî si hî.	فِى كِيسِهِ .
The foreigner customer	az za bön al''aaj na bî	اَلزَّبُونُ الاجنبى
looks at	yan zö rö 'ai lã	يَنظُرُ الى
the cashier	'aa mîni_S_ _S_ön döq	أمينِ الصُّندُوق
and he says to him :	wa ya qö lö la hð:	ويَقُولُ لَه :
Thank you brother	Šök ran yã 'aa _Kî._	شُكراً يَاأخى .
Cashier:	'aa mî nö_S_ _S_ön döq:	أمينُ الصُّندُوق:
Mention not,	a'af wan,	عَفُواً،
no thanks	lã Šök ra	لَا شُكر
for duty.	a'a lã wã jib.	علىٰ واجب .
We are always	na_H_ nö dã 'ai man	نَحنُ دَائِماً
at your service.	fî _K_id ma tik.	فِى خِدمتِك .
The customer leaves	ya_K_ rö jöz za bön	يَخرُجُ الزَّبُون
the bank	mi nal bank	مِنَ البنك
and he heads	wa ya ta waj ja hö	ويَتَوَجَّه
to his hotel.	'ai la fön dö qi hî.	الى فُندِقِه .

94

Exercise

التمرين

Question (1)

السؤال(١)

what does the foreigner
customer want?

mã Đã yö rî döz za
bồn al 'aaj na bî?

مَاذَايُرِيدُ
الزَّبُونُ الاجنبى ؟

Answer

الجواب

The foreigner customer
wants

az za bồ nöl 'aaj na bî
yö rîd

اَلزَّبُونُ الاَجنَبى
يُرِيدُ

to change his currency

tab dîl a'öm la ti hî.

تَبْدِيل عُمْلَته .

Question (2)

السؤال(٢)

What does the hotel clerk
say to him ?

mã Đã ya qồ lö la hö
kã ti böl fồn döq?

مَاذَا يَقُولُ لَه
كَاتبُ الفُندُق؟

Answer

الجواب

The hotel clerk
tells him:

ya qồl la hö kã ti böl
fồn döq:

يَقُولُ له كَاتب
الفُندق :

Sir,

yã say yi dî,

يَاسَيِّدى ،

we have

yồ ja dö la day nã

يُوجَدُ لَدَينا

this facility.

hã Đi his sö hồ la.

هذه السَّهُولة.

What do you have?

mã Đã a'in dak?

مَاذَا عِندَك ؟

Question (3)

السؤال(٣)

English	Transliteration	Arabic
What does the customer tell the clerk?	mã Đã ya qð löz za bõn lil kã tib ?	مَاذَا يَقُولُ الزَّبُون لِلكَاتِب ؟
Answer		الجواب
The customer says:	ya qð löz za bon:	يَقُول الزَّبُون :
I have dollars.	a'in dî dð lã rãt .	عِندى دولارات
Question (4)		السؤال(٤)
What does the clerk say to the customer?	mã Đã ya qð löl kã tib liz za bõn?	مَاذَا يَقُولُ الكَاتِب لِلزَّبُون ؟
Answer:		الجواب
The clerk says:	ya qð löl kã tib:	يَقُولُ الكَاتِب :
Sorry sir,	'aã sif yã say yi dî,	آسِف يَاسَيِّدى ،
we don't have	mã a'in da nã	مَاعِندنا
today's rate	sia' röl yawm	سِعرُ اليوم
of dollar.	lid dð lãr.	للدُولار.
You may go	möm kin taĐ hab	مُمكِن تَذهَب
to	'ai lal	الى
the Central Bank.	ban kil mar ka zî?	البَنْكِ المَركَزى.
Question (5)		السؤال(٥)
Does the customer go	hal yaĐ ha böz za bõn	هَلُ يَذهبُ الزَّبُون
to	'ai lal	الى

96

the Central bank?	ban kil mar kazî?	البَنْكِ المَركَزى؟
Answer		الجواب
Yes,	na a'am,	نَعَمُ ،
the customer goes	yaÐ ha böz za bðn	يَذهَبُ الزَّبون
to	'ai lal	الى
the Central bank	ban kil mar ka zî	البَنْكِ المَركَزى
and exchanges	wa yö bad dî lö	وِيُبَدِّلُ
one hundred dollars.	mi 'aat dð lãr.	مِئَةَ دُولاَر.

❰☆☆☆☆❱

Lesson 15

Numerals

العدد

one	wã Hid	وَاجِد ١
two	'aiT nãn	اثْنَان ٢
three	Ta lã Ta	ثَلاثَة ٣
four	'aar ba a'a	أَرْبَعَة ٤
five	Kam sa	خُمْسَة ٥
six	sit ta	سِتَّة ٦
seven	sab a'a	سَبْعَة ٧
eight	Ta mã ni ya	ثَمَانِية ٨
nine	tis a'a	تِسْعَة ٩
ten	a'a Ša ra	عَشَرَة ١٠
elevan	'aa Ha da a'a Ša ra	أَحَدَ عَشَرَ ١١
twelve	'aiT nã a'a Ša ra	اثْنَا عَشَرَ ١٢
thirteen	Ta lã Ta ta a'a Ša ra	ثَلاثَة عَشَرَ ١٣
fourteen	'aar ba a'a ta a'a Ša ra	اربَعَة عَشَرَ ١٤
fifteen	Kam sa ta a'a Ša ra	خُمْسَة عَشَرَ ١٥
sixteen	sit ta ta a'a Ša ra	سِتَّة عَشَرَ ١٦
senventeen	sab a'a ta a'a Ša ra	سَبْعَة عَشَرَ ١٧
	Ta mã ni ya ta a'a Šara	ثَمَانِية عَشَرَ ١٨

98

nineteen	tis a'a ta a'a Ša ra	تِسعَة عَشَرَ ١٩
twenty	a'iŠ rðn	عِشرُون ٢٠
thirty	Ta lã Tðn	ثَلاثُون ٣٠
forty	'aar ba a'ðn	أُربَعُون ٤٠
fifry	Kam sðn	خَمسُون ٥٠
sixty	sit tðn	سِتُّون ٦٠
seventy	sab a'ðn	سَبعُون ٧٠
eighty	Ta mã nðn	ثَمَانُون ٨٠
ninety	tis a'ðn	تِسعُون ٩٠
hundered	mi 'aa	مئة ١٠٠
thousand	'aalf	أَلَف ١٠٠٠
twenty one	wã Hid wa a'iŠ rðn	وَاحِد وَعِشرُونَ ٢١
twenty two	'aiT nã ni wa a'iŠ rðn	اثنَان وَعِشرُونَ ٢٢
twenty three	Ta lã Ta wa a'iŠ rðn	ثَلاثَة وَعِشرُونَ ٢٣
ninety nine	tis a'a tön wa tis a'ðn	تِسعَة وَتِسعُون ٩٩
one thousand one hundred	'aal fön wa mi 'aa	أَلَف وَمِئَة ١١٠٠

| This is Jawahar Lal Nehru University. | hã Ði hi jã mi a'at ja wã har lãl nih rð. | هَذه جَامِعة جَوَاهَر لال نهرو. |
| It is big. | hi ya ka bî ra tön. | هِى كَبِيرَةٌ. |

English	Transliteration	Arabic
It has	fî hã	فِيهَا
five faculties	Kam sö köl lî yã tin.	خَمْسُ كُلِّيَات.
including:	min hã:	مِنهَا
school of languages.	köl lî ya töl lö ghãt.	كُلِّيَةُ اللُّغَات.
There are three	hö nãk Ta lã Ta tö	هُنَاك ثَلاثَةُ
storeys	'aad wãr	ادوار
for the school of	li köl lî ya til	لِكُلِّيَةِ
languages.	lö ghãt.	اللُّغَات.
Each floor has	fî köl li dawr	فِى كُلِّ دَور
thirty three	Ta lã Ta tön wa	ثَلاثَة وَ ثَلاثُون
rooms.	Ta lã Tö na ghör fatan.	غُرفَةً.
I teach	'aa nã 'ad rös	أَنَا ادرُس
the French Language.	al löghatal fö ran sî ya.	اَللُّغَةَ الفَرَنسِيَّة
There are	hö nãk	هُنَاك
fifteen	Kam sa ta a'a Ša ra	خَمْسَةَ عَشَرَ
teachers in	mö dar ri san fil	مُدَرِّساً فِى
the French Language.	lö gha til fö ran sî ya.	اللُّغَةِ الفَرَنسِيَّة
There are	hö nãk	هُنَاك
twenty five	Kamsatön waa'iŠ rðna	خَمْسَة وعِشرون
boys	wa ladan	وَلَداً

English	Transliteration	Arabic
in my class.	fî fa_S_ lî.	فِى فَصْلِى
In another class	wa fî fa_S_ lin 'aã <u>Kar</u>	وَفِى فَصل آخر
there are	hö nãk	هُنَاك
twenty five	<u>k</u>am sön wa a'i<u>Š</u> rð na	خَمْسٌ وَعِشْرُون
girls.	bin tan.	بِنْتاً.
We are all	na_H_ nö köl lö nã	نَحْنُ كُلُّنَا
in the French Language	fil lö ghatil fö ran sî ya	فِى اللُّغَةِ الفَرَنْسِيَّة
one hundred boys and	mi 'aat wa la din	مِئَة وَلَد و
one hundred girls.	wa mi 'aat bin tin.	مِئَة بِنْت.
In the school of languages	wa fî köllî ya til lö ghãt	وَفِى كُلِّيَةِ اللُّغَات
we are one thousand	na_H_ nö 'aal fö	نَحْنُ اَلْفُ
boys and girls.	wa la din wa bin tin.	وَلَد وَبِنْت.
In each language	fî köl li lö gha tin	فِى كُلِّ لُغَة
there are about hundred	mi'aatön wa <u>K</u>am sö̃na	مِئَة وَخَمْسُون
and fifty boys	wa la dan wa bin tan	وَلَداً وَبِنتاً
and girls.	taq rî ban.	تَقْرِيباً.

Exercise

التمرين

Question (1)

السؤال (١)

How many faculties	kam köl lî ya tan	كم كُلِّيَّةً
are there in the Jawhar lal	fî jã mi a'a ti ja wã har	فى جامعة جواهر
Nehru University?	lãl nih rð?	لال نهرو؟

Answer

الجواب

There are five	hö nãk <u>Kam</u> sö	هُنَاك خمسُ
faculties	köl lî yã tin	كُلِّيَّاتٍ
in the Jawharlal Nehru	fî jã mi a'at ja wã har	فى جامعة جواهر
University.	lãl nih rð.	لال نهرو.

Question (2)

السؤال (٢)

How many storeys	kam daw ran	كم دَوراً
are there in the School of	fî	فى
languages?	köl lî ya til lö ghãt?	كُلِّيَّة اللغات؟

Answer

الجواب

There are five storeys/	hö nãk <u>Kam</u> sö	هناك خَمسُ
floor for the school	'aad wã rin	أدوار لكلية
of languages.	li köl lî ya til lö ghãt	اللغات

Question (3)

السؤال (٣)

| How many rooms | Kam ghör fa tan | كَمْ غُرفَةً |

102

are there in	fî	فى
each floor?	köl li daw rin?	كُلِّ دَورٍ
Answer		الجواب
There are fifteen	hö nãk <u>K</u>am sa ta	هناك خَمسة
rooms	a'a Ša ra ghör fa tan	عشر غرفةً
in each floor.	fî köl li dawr.	في كُلِّ دَورٍ.
Question (4)		السؤال (٤)
How many teachers	kam mö dar ri san	كمْ مُدرِّساً
are there in the	fil lö gha til	فى اللغة
French language?	fö ran sî ya?	الفَرنسية؟
Answer		الجواب
There are	hö nãk	هُناك
fifteen	<u>K</u>am sa ta a'a Ša ra	خمسة عَشر
teachers	mö dar ri san	مُدرِّساً
in the	fil lö gha til	في اللُّغةِ
French language.	fö ran sî ya.	الفُرَنسيةَ
Question (5)		السؤال (٥)
How many boys	kam wa la dan	كمْ وَلَداً
are there in	fî	فى
your class?	fa<u>S</u> lik?	فصلك؟

English	Transliteration	Arabic
Answer		الجواب
There are	hö nãk	هُناك
twenty five	Kam sa tön wa	خمسةٌ و
boys	a'iŠ rð na wa la dan	عشرون وَلداً
in my class.	fî fa_S_ lî.	فى فضُلي
Question (6)		السؤال (٦)
How many students are	kam ťã li ban	كم طَالبا
there	hö nãk	هناك
in the faculty	fî köl lîya til	في كُليَّة
of languages?	lö ghãt?	اللغات؟
(school of languages)		
Answer		الجواب
There are	hö nãk	هُناك
one thousand	'aal fö wa la din	الف ولدٍ
boys and girls	wa bin tin	و بنتٍ
in the	fî	فى
school of languages.	köl lîya til lö ghãt.	كلية اللغات.

❖☆☆☆❖

Lesson 16

أيام الأسبوع

Conversation		محادثة
A week	ya ta kaw wa nö	يَتَكَوَّنُ
comprises	'aös bða'	أُسْبُوع
seven days.	minsaba'ati 'aayyãmin.	مِنْ سَبْعَةِ أيّام .
They are Saturday	wa hi ya yaw mös sabt	وَهِى يَومُ السَبت
Sunday	wa yaw möl 'aa Had	وَيَومُ الأَحَد
Monday	wa yaw möl 'aiT nayn	وَيَومُ الاثنَين
Tuesday	wayawmöT Tö lã Tã'a	وَيَومُ الثُّلاثَاء
Wednesday	wa yawmöl 'aarbi a'ã'ai	وَيَومُ الاربِعَاء
Thursday	wa yaw möl Ka mîs	وَيَومُ الخَمِيس
and Friday.	wa yaw möljöm a'a.	وَيَومُ الجُمعَة .
We in India	naH nö fil hind	نَحنُ فى الهِند
work for five	naa' ma lö li Kam sa ti	نَعمَل لِخَمسَةِ
days in the	'aay yã min fil	أيَّام فى
government offices.	makã ti bil Hökö mîya.	المَكَاتِب الحُكُومِيّة .
They are,	wa hi ya :	وَهِى :
Monday	yaw möl 'aiT nayn	يَوم الاثنَين
Tuesday	wa yawmöT Tölã Tã 'a	وَيَومُ الثُّلاثَاء

105

English	Transliteration	Arabic
Wednesday	wa yawmöl 'aar bia'ā'a	وَيَومُ الاربِعَاء
Thursday	wa yaw möl Ka mîs	وَيَومُ الخَمِيس
and Friday.	wa yaw möl jöm a'a.	وَيَومُ الجُمعة .
As regards	'am mã fî	أمَّا فى
Saturdays	ay yã mis sabt	أيَّام السبت
and Sundays,	wal 'aa Had	والأَحَد
we are on	na kð nö fî	نَكُونُ فى
official holidays	'ai jã za tin ras mîyatin	إجَازَةٍ رَسمِيَّةٍ
each week.	köl la 'aös bða'.	كُلُّ أسبُوعٍ .
In these two days	fî hã Ðayn alyawmayn	فى هذين اليَومَين
workers of the	yök mi löl a'ã mi lðn fil	يُكمِلُ العَامِلُون فى
government offices finish	ma kã ti bil Hö kð mi ya	المَكاتِب الحُكُومِيَّة
their	a'aa' mã la höm	أعمَالَهُم
personal work	al KãS Sa	الخَاصَّة
and go out for	wa yaK rö jð na fî	وَيَخرُجُونَ فى
family outings.	nöz hã tin a'ã 'ai lîyatin.	نزهَاتٍ عَائِليَّةٍ .
We find in	na ji dö fî	نَجِدُ فى
these two days	hã Ðay nil yaw mayn	هَذَين اليَومَين
all the	köl lal Ha dã 'ai qil	كُلّ الحَدَائِق
public gardens	a'ãm ma	العَامَّة

106

English	Transliteration	Arabic
full of people.	ma lî 'aa tan bin nãs	مَلِيئَةً بِالنَاسِ.
We also find	wa ka Đã lik na ji dö	وَكَذَلِك نَجِدُ
the cinema halls	dð ral Ka yãl	دُورَالخَيَالِ
full of	ma lî 'aa tan	مَلِيئَةً
spectators of	bil mö ta far ri jîn	بِالمُتَفَرِّجِينَ
the movies.	a'a lal 'aaflãm.	عَلىْ الأَفْلَام.
In these two days	fî HãÐaynil yawmayni	فِى هَذين اليومين
the office goers	yaK rö jöl a'ã mi lðn	يَخرُجُ العَامِلُونَ فِى
also go	fil ma kã tib 'aay dan	المَكَاتِب أيضاً
out visiting	fî zi yã rã tin	فِى زِيَارَاتٍ
their friends	li 'aaS di qã 'ai him	لأَصْدِقَائِهم
and relatives.	wa 'aaq ri bã 'ai him.	وَأقرِبَائِهم.
However, on the rest of	'aam mã fî baqî ya	أمَّا فِى بَقِيَّة
five days	til 'aay ya mil Kam sa	الأَيَّام الخَمسَة
they work	höm yaa' ma lð na	هُم يَعمَلُونَ
in their offices	fî ma kã ti bi him	فِى مَكَاتِبِهم
from 9.00	mi nas sã a'a tit tã si	مِنَ السَاعَةِ التَاسِعَةِ
A.M.	a'a Sa bã Han 'ai las	صَبَاحَاً الى
to 5.00	sã a'a til Kã mi sa	السَاعَة الخَامِسَةِ
P.M. regularly.	ma sã 'aan bin ti zãm.	مَسَاءً بِانتِظام.

English	Transliteration	Arabic
We find offices thronged	na ji döl ma kã ti ba	نَجِدُ المَكَاتِبَ
by office workers	ma lî'aa tan bila'ömmãl	مَلِيئَةً بالعُمَّالِ
and the visitors on	waz zŏw wãr fî	والزُوَّارِ فى
these days.	hã Đi hil 'aay yãm.	هَذه الايَّامِ.
They finish the official	yök mi lŏ nal 'aaa' mã	يُكمِلُونَ الأعمَالَ
work.	lar r'as mî ya.	الرسمية.

Exercise — التمرين

Question (1) — السؤال (١)

English	Transliteration	Arabic
How many days are there in a week?	kam yaw man fî 'aös bða' ?	كَمْ يَومًا فى أُسُبُوعٍ؟

Answer — الجواب

English	Transliteration	Arabic
There are seven days in a week	hö nãk sab a'a tö 'aay yã min fî 'aös bða'.	هُنَاكَ سَبْعةُ أيام فى أسبُوع.

Question (2) — السؤال (٢)

English	Transliteration	Arabic
Do you remember the names of the week days?	hal taĐ kö rö 'aas mã 'aa 'aay yã mil 'aös bða' ?	هَل تَذكُرُ أسمَاءَ أيَّام الاسُبُوع؟

Answer — الجواب

English	Transliteration	Arabic
Yes, they are:	na 'aam, hi ya	نَعَمُ، هى

English	Transliteration	Arabic
Saturday	yaw mös sabt	يَومُ السَّبت
Sunday	yaw möl 'aa *H*ad	يَومُ الأَحَد
Monday	yaw möl 'ai*T* nayn	يَومُ الاثنين
Tuesday	yaw mö*T T*ö lã *T*ã'a	يَومُ الثُّلَاثَاء
Wednesday	yaw möl 'aar bi a'ã'a	يَومُ الارْبِعَاء
Thursday	yaw möl <u>K</u>a mîs	يَومُ الخَميس
and Friday.	wa yaw möl jöm a'a.	وَيَومُ الجُمعَة.

Question (3) السؤال (٣)

How many days	kam yaw man	كَم يَومًا
in a week /per week	fil 'aös bö a'i	فى الأسُبُوع
do we work	naa' ma lö	نَعْمَلُ
in India?	fil hind?	فى الهِندِ؟

Answer الجواب

We work in India	naa' ma lö fil hind	نَعمَل فِى الهِنْد
for five days	li <u>K</u>am sati 'aay yãmin	لِخَمسَةِ أَيَّام
in a week /per week	fî 'aös böa'.	فى أسبوع.

Question (4) السؤال (٤)

When do the office	ma tã ya<u>K</u> rö jöl	مَتىٰ يَخرُجُ
workers in India leave/	a'ã mi lö na fil	العَامِلُون فى
go out	ma kã tib fil hind	المَكَاتِب فى الهِندِ

109

for picnic?	lin nöz ha?	لِلنُزهَة؟
Answer		الجواب
Officegoers	yaK rö jöl a'ã mi lð na	يَخرُجُ الغَامِلُون
in India go out	fil hind	فى الهند
for picnic	lin nöz ha	للنزهة
on Saturdays	fî 'aay yã mis sab ti	فى أيّام السبت
& Sundays.	wal 'aa Had.	و الاحد.
Question (5)		السؤال (٥)
How do we find	kay fa na ji döl	كَيفَ نَجِدُ
the public gardens	Ha dã 'ai qal a'ãm ma	الحَدَائِقَ الغَامَّةَ
and cinema halls	wa dð ral Ka yãl	وَدُورَالخَيَالِ
on Saturdays	fî 'aay yã mis sab ti	فى أيّام السبت
and Sundays?	wal 'aa Had ?	والأحد؟
Answer		الجواب
We find the public	na ji döl Ha dã 'ai qal	نَجِدُ الحَدَائِق
gardens and	a'ãm ma wa	الغَامَّةَ وَ
Cinema halls	dð ral Ka yãl	دُورَالخَيَالِ
full of people	ma lî 'aa tan bin nãs	مَلِيئَةً بالنَّاسِ
on Saturdays	fî 'aay yã mis sab ti	فى أيّامِ السَّبُت
and Sundays.	wal 'aa Had.	والأحَد.

◆☆☆☆◆

Lesson 17

Conversation		محادثة
Abdullah is	a'ab döl lãh	عَبْدُاللَّه
from Egypt.	min miSr.	مِن مِصر.
He is a trader /businessman.	hö wã tã jir.	هُو تَاجِرٌ.
Abdullah travels	yö sã fir a'ab döl lãh	يُسافِر عبدُالله
from country	min ba la din	مِن بَلَدٍ
to country	'ai lã ba la din	الىٰ بَلَدٍ
for business work.	fî'aaa' mã lin ti jã rî ya.	فى أعمَالٍ تِجَارِية.
He travels	hö wa yö sã fî rö	هُو يُسَافِر
by air mostly /most of the occasions.	bi† †ã 'ai ra ti fî 'aagh la bil 'aaH yãn.	بِالطائِرةِ فى أغلَبِ الأَحيان.
Once Abdullah travelled	mar ra tan sã fa ra a'ab döl lãh	مَرَّةً سَافَر عَبْدُالله
from Cairo,	mi nal qã hi ra	مِن القَاهِرة
the capital of Egypt	a'ã Si mat miSr	عَاصِمةِ مصر
to New Delhi,	'ai lã nî yð dil hî	الى نيودلهى
the capital of India.	a'ã Si ma til hind.	عَاصِمَةِ الهند.
When the aeroplane	a'in da mã wa Sa la	عِندَمَاوَصَلت

111

English	Transliteration	Arabic
reached	tit̩ t̩ã 'ai ra	الطَّائِرَةُ
New Delhi airport,	ma t̩ã ra nî yð dil hî	مَطَار نيودلهى
Abdullah got down	ha ba t̩a a'ab döl lãh	هَبَطَ عَبدُالله
from the aeroplane,	mi nat̩ t̩a 'ai ra ti	مِنَ الطَّائِرَةِ
and headed towards	wa ta waj ja ha 'ai lã	وَتَوَجَّه الى
the arrival hall	S̲ã la til wö S̲ðl	صَالةِ الوُصُول
to take/collect his	li ya'a K̲ö Ða	لِيَأخُذَ
baggage.	a'a fa Ša hð.	عَفَشَه.
His friend	kã na S̲a dî qö hð	كَانَ صَدِيقُه
Sundar was	sðn dãr	سوندار
waiting for him	fin ti z̲ã ri hi	فى إنْتِظَارِه
in the waiting hall.	fi S̲ã la til 'ain ti z̲ãr.	فى صَالةِالانتَظار.
Abdullah took	'aa K̲a Ða a'ab döl lãh	أخَذَ عبد الله
his baggage from the	a'a fa Ša hö min	عَفشَه من
baggage belt	H̲i z̲ã mil a'a faŠ	جِزَام العَفَش
and headed	wa ta waj ja ha	وَتَوَجَّه
for the customs.	lil ja mã rik.	لِلجَمارك:
The customs	'aaa' t̩ã hö	أعطَاه
officer gave him the	mö waz̲ z̲a föl ja mã rik	مُوَظَّف الجَمَارك
arrival card.	bi t̩ã qa tal wö S̲ðl	بِطَاقةَ الوُصُولِ.

They had the	wa ja rã bay na hö mã	وَجَرَى بينَهما
following conversation:	al Ha dî Tat tã lî:	الحَدِيثُ التَّالى :
Customs officer:	mö waz za föl ja mãrik:	مُوَظَّفُ الجَمَارِك:
Sir,	say yi dî,	سَيِّدى ،
where are you from?	min 'aay na 'aan ta?	مِنْ أين أنت؟
Fill up this card/	'aim la'a hã Ði hil bi†ãqa	إملأ هذه البطَاقة
please.	min fadlik.	مِن فَضلِك.
Abdullh:	a'ab döl lãh:	عَبدُالله:
Brother, I am	yã 'aa Kî, 'aa nã	يَا أخى ،أنا
from Egypt.	min miSr.	مِن مِصر.
I am an Egyptian.	'aa nã miS rî.	أنَا مِصرى.
Abdullah fills up	yam la 'aö a'ab döl lãh	يَمْلأ عبدالله
the arrival card,	bi †ã qa tal wö Sõl,	بطَاقةَ الوُصُول،
and hands it over	wa yö sal li mö hã	وَيُسَلِّمُها
to the officer.	lil mö waz zaf.	لِلمُوَظَّفِ.
Customs officer:	mö waz za föl ja mãrik:	مُوَظَّفُ الجَمَارِك:
Where is your passport,	'aay na ja wãz sa farik	أينَ جَوازُ سَفَرِك
respected sir?	yã sayyidîl möHtaram?	يَاسَيِّدى المُحْتَرَم؟
Abdullah:	a'ab döl lãh :	عَبدُاللَّه:
Here is my passport.	hã Ðã ja wãz sa fa rî.	هذَا جَوازُ سَفَرى.

Customs officer:	mo waz za föl ja mãrik:	مُوَظَّفُ الجَمَارِك:
Where are	min 'aay na	مِنْ أَينَ
you coming from now?	'aan ta qã di mön al'aãn?	أَنتَ قَادِمٌ الآن ؟
Abdullah:	a'ab döl lãh: 'aa nã	عَبْدُاللَّه: أَنا
I am coming now	qã di mön al 'aã na	قَادِمٌ الآن
from Egypt	mi nal qã hi ra	مِنَ القَاهِرة
directly.	mö bã Ša ra tan.	مُبَاشَرَةً ،
Customs officer:	mö waz za föl ja mãrik:	مُوَظَّفُ الجَمَارِك:
What is the purpose of	mã sa bab	مَاسَبَبُ
your visit to	zi yã ra tik	زِيَارَتِك
New Delhi?	li ni yð dil hî?	لنيودلهى؟
Abdullah:	a'ab döl lãh:	عَبْدُ اللَّه :
I am a trader/	'aa nã tã jir.	أَنَا تَاجِرٌ.
businessman.		
I came to	ji'a tö 'ai lã	جِئتُ الى
New Delhi.	ni yð dil hî	نيودلهى
for business.	li 'aaa' mã lin ti jã rî ya.	لِأعمالٍ تجارِيَّة.
Customs officer:	mo waz za föl ja mãrik:	مُوَظَّفُ الجَمَارِك:
What is your address	mã a'ön wã nök	مَاعنوانُك
in New Delhi?	fî nî yð dil hî?	فى نيودلهى؟

114

Abdullah:	a'ab döl lãh:	عَبْدُاللَّه :
I'll stay with	sa 'aö qî mö ma a'a *S*a	سَأُقِيمُ مَعَ
a friend of mine	dîqin lî	صَديق لى
and my colleague in work	wa za mî lî fil a'a mal	وَزَميلى فِى العَملِ
(confrer) Sundar,	sön dãr	سوندار
in Munirka,	fî mð nîr kã,	فِى مونيركا ،
New Delhi.	nî yð dil hî.	نيودلهى .
Customs officer:	mö waz za föl ja mãrik:	مُوَظَّفُ الجَمَارِك:
How many days will you	kam yaw man sa töqîm	كَم يَوماً سَتُقِيمُ
stay in New Delhi?	fî nî yð dil hî?	فِى نيودلهى ؟
Perhaps I would need	röb ba mã 'aa*H* tã jö'ailã	رُبَّمَا أحتَاجُ الى
to extend my stay	tam dîd 'ai qã ma tî	تَمديد اقامَتى
for another week.	li 'aös bða' 'aã *K*ar.	لأسبُوع آخر.
Where should I	'aay na yöm ki nö lî	أينَ يُمكِنُ لى
go to renew	'aaÐ hab li taj dîd	أذهبُ لِتَجديد
my visa?	ta'a Šî ra tî ?	تَأشِيرتى ؟
Customs officer:	mö waz za föl ja mãrik:	مُوَظَّفُ الجَمَارِك:
Sir,	say yi dî,	سَيِّد ى ،
you have to go	yal zam 'aaÐ Ða hãb	يَلزَمُ الذَّهاب
to the passport and	'ai lãmak ta bil jawã	الى مَكتبِ الجَوازَاتِ

115

emigration office	zãt wal hij ra	والهِجرَة
for this work.	lihã Ði hil a'a ma lî ya.	لهذه العَمليّة.
Abdullah: Thanks.	a'ab döl lãh : Šök ran.	عَبدُ اللّه: شُكراً.
Customs officer:	mö waz za föl ja mãrik:	مُوَظّفُ الجَمَارِك:
Do you have	hal a'in dak	هَل عِندَك
customable	'aaŠ yã 'aö qã bi la	أشياء قَابِلةٌ
items?	lil jöm rök?	للجمرك؟
Abdullah	a'ab döl lãh:	عَبدُاللّه:
No, brother.	lã, yã 'aa Kî .	لَا، ياأخى.
Customs officer :	mo waz za föl ja mãrik:	مُوَظّفُ الجَمَارِك:
Open your box	'aif taH Sön dð qak	افتَحُ صُندوقَك ،
please.	min fad lik.	مِن فَضلِك.
Abdullah opens	yaf ta Hö a'ab döl lãh	يَفتَحُ عَبدُاللّه
his box	Sön dð qa hð	صُندوقَه
and the customs officer	wa yö fat ti Šö hö	وَيُفتِّشُه
cheks it.	möwaz za föl ja mãrik. .	مُوَظّفُ الجَمَارِك ..
The customs officer	lã ya ji dö fî hi	لايَجِدُ فيه
did not find in it	mö waz za föl ja mãrik	مُوَظّفُ الجَمَارِك
anything	Šay 'aan yaa' ta ri dö	شَيئاً يَعتَرِضُ
objectionable.	a'al ay hi.	عليه.

116

He permits him	fa yas ma _H_ö la hö	فَيَسمَحُ له
to close the box	bi 'aigh lã qi_S_ _S_ön dõq	بِاغلاقِ الصُّندوقِ
and to leave.	wal _K_ö rðj.	وَالخُروج.
Abdullah takes	a'ab döl lãh ya'a _K_öÐö	عَبُدُاللَّه يَاخُذُ
his box and leaves	_S_ön dõ qa hö wa ya_K_	صُندُوقَه وَيَخرُجُ
the arrival hall	rö jö min_S_ã la til wö_S_ðl	مِنْ صَالِةِالوُصُول
for the waiting hall.	'ai lã _S_ã la til 'ain ti _z_ãr	الىٰ صَالِةِ الانتظار
There he finds	wa ya ji dö hö nãk	وَيَجِدُ هناك
his friend Sundar	_S_a dî qa hö sön dãr	صَديقَه سوندار
waiting for him.	fin ti _z_ã ri hi.	فى انتظَاره.
The two leave	al 'ai_T_ nã ni ya_K_ rö jãni	الاثنَان يَخرُجَان
together	sə wî yan	سَويًّا
and take	wa ya'a _K_ö dã ni	وَيأخُذَان
a taxi for home.	tãk siy yan 'ai lal bayt.	تاكسيا الى البَيت.

Exercise   التمرين

Question (1)   السؤال (١)

who is Abdullah?	man hö wa a'ab döllãh?	مِنْ هُو عَبُدُاللَّه ؟
Answer		الجواب
Abdullh is an Eyptian.	a'ab döl lãh mi_S_ rî.	عَبُدُاللَّه مِصريٌّ.

117

Question (2)		السؤال (٢)
What is Abdullah's profession?	mã hi ya mih na tö a'ab döl lãh?	مَاهِى مِهْنَةُ عَبد اللَّه ؟
Answer		الجواب
Abdullah is trader /businessman.	a'ab döl lãh tã jir.	عَبدُاللَّه تَاجِرٌ
Question (3)		السؤال (٣)
How does Abdullah travel most of the time?	kay fa yö sã fir a'ab döl lãh fi 'aagh labil 'aaH yãn?	كَيف يُسَافِرُ عَبدُاللَّه فى أغلَبِ الأحيان؟
Answer		الجواب
Abdullah travels most of the times by air.	yö sã fir rö a'ab döl lãh fi 'aagh la bil 'aaH yãn bi† †ã 'ai ra.	يُسَافِر عَبدُاللَّه فِى أغلَبِ الاحيان بِالطَّائِرة ۔
Question (4)		السؤال (٤)
What did the customs officer give him on his arrival in New Delhi?	mã Đã 'aaa' tã hö mö waz za föl ja mãrik la dã wö Sõ li hi 'ai lã ni yõ dil hî ?	مَاذَا أَعطَاه مُوَظَّفُ الجَمَارِك لَدىٰ وُصُولِه الى نيودلهى؟

118

English	Transliteration	Arabic
Answer		الجواب
The customs officer gave	'aaa' †ã hö	أعطاه
him	mö wa<u>z</u> <u>za</u> föl ja mãrik	مُوَظَّفُ الجَمَارِك
an arrival card	bi †ã qa ta wö <u>S</u>ől	بِطَاقَةَ وُصُول
on his arrival	la dã wö <u>S</u>ð li hî	لَدىٰ وُصُوله
in New Delhi.	ni yð dil hî.	نيودلهى.
Question (5)		السؤال (٥)
What did the customs	mã Ðã qã la la hö	مَاذَا قَالَ له
officer say	mö wa<u>z</u> <u>za</u> föl	مُوَظَّفُ
to him?	ja mãrik?	الجَمَارِك؟
Answer		الجواب
The customs officer	mö wa<u>z</u> <u>za</u> föl ja mãrik	مُوَظَّفُ الجَمَارِك
asked him a few	sa 'aa la hö a'id da ta	سَأَلَه عِدةَ
questions	'aas 'ai la tin	أسئِلةٍ
about the purpose of his	Haw la sa bab	حَولَ سَبَبِ
visit	zi yã ra ti hî	زِيَارَته
to New Delhi.	li nî yð dil hî .	لِنيودلهى.
Question (6)		السؤال(٦)
Will Abdullah stay in a	hal sa yö qî mö	هَلْ سَيُقِيمُ
hotel?	a'abdöl lãh bi fön döq?	عَبدُاللَّه بِفُندق؟

English	Transliteration	Arabic
Answer		الجواب
No, Abdullah	lã, a'ab döl lãh	لَا، عَبْدُاللَّه
will stay in	sa yö qîmö fî	سَيُقِيمُ فى
New Delhi with	nî yð dil hî ma a'a _Sa_	نيودلهى مَع
his friend Sundar	dî qi hi Sðn dãr.	صَدِيقه سوندار.
Question (7)		السؤال (٧)
Where does	'aay na yas kö nö	أينَ يَسكُنُ
Sundar live?	Sðn dãr?	سوندار؟
Answer		الجواب
Sundar lives	yas kö nö Sðn dar	يَسكُنُ سوندار
in Munirka	fî mð nîr kã	فى مونيركا
in New Delhi.	fî ni yð dil hî.	فى نيودلهى.
Question (8)		السؤال (٨)
How many days	kam yaw man sayöqîm	كَمْ يَومًاسَيُقِيم
Abdullah will stay in	a'ab döl lãh fî	عَبْدُاللَّه فى
New Delhi?	ni yð dil hî?	نيودلهى ؟
Answer		الجواب
Abdullah has	a'in da a'ab döl lãh	عِندَ عَبدُ اللَّه
2-week visa.	ta'a Šî ra tö'aös bða'ayn.	تَأشِيرُة أسبُوعَين.
He might renew it	röb ba mã yöjaddid hã	رُبَّمَا يُجَدِّدُهَا

120

for another week.	li 'aös bð a'in 'aã <u>K</u>ar.	لِأسبُوعٍ آخر.
Question (9)		السؤال (٩)
Do you like to travel by air?	hal to *H*ib bös sa fa ra bi† †ã 'ai ra?	هَلْ تُحِبُّ السَفَرَ بِالطَّائِرةِ ؟
Answer		الجواب
Yes, I like	na a'am, 'aö *H*ib bös	نَعَمْ، أُحِبُّ
to travel by air.	sa far bi† †ã 'ai ra.	السَفَرَ بِالطَّائِرة.
But the travel	wa lã kin nas sa fa ra	وَلْكِنَّ السَّفَرَ
by train	bil qi †ãr	بِالقِطَارِ
is more interesting.	möm tia' 'aak *T*ar.	مُمتِعٌ أكثَر.

❖☆☆☆❖

121

Coversation   محادثة

This is my watch,	hã Đi hi sã a'a tî.	هَذه سَاعَتِى.
This watch is	hã Đi hi sã a'a tön	هَذه سَاعَةٌ
beautiful.	ja mî la tön.	جَمِيلَةٌ.
I took this	'aa KaĐ tö hã Đi his	أَخَذْتُ هَذه
watch	sã a'a ta	السَاعةَ
from my elder brother	min 'aa Kî al ka bîr	مِنْ أَخِى الكَبِير
Abdur Rahman	a'ab dör raH mãn	عَبْدالرَّحمْن
after my success	baa' da na jã Hî	بَعدَ نَجَاحِى
in the final	fil 'aim ti Hãn	فِى الامتِحَانِ
examination.	al 'aa Kîr.	الاخِير.
I wear	'aal ba sö	أَلْبَسُ
this watch	hã Đi his sã a'a ta	هَذه السَاعة
when I leave	a'in da mã a'aK röjö	عِندمَا أَخْرُجُ
the house	mi nal bay ti	مِنَ البَيتِ
for the the school.	lil mad ra sa.	لِلمَدرَسَةِ.
This watch	tö sã a'i dö nî	تُسَاعِدُنى
helps me	hã Đi his sã a'a tö	هذه السَاعة
in finishing my work	fî 'ain jã zi 'aaa' mã lî	فِى انجَازِ أَعْمَالِى

122

on fixed	fî 'aaw qã tin	فِى أَوقَاتٍ
times.	mö Had da da.	مُحَدَّدَةٍ.
My brother taught me	a'al la ma nî 'aa Kî	عَلَّمَنِى أَخِى
to know time	maa' ri fa taz za man	مَعرِفَة الزَّمنِ
from it.	bi hã.	بِها .
He taught me	a'al la ma nî	عَلَّمَنى
that the second	'aan naT Tã ni ya ta	أَنَّ الثَانِيَةَ
is the smallest part	'aaS gha rö jöz 'ain	أَصغَرُ جُزءٍ
of time.	mi naz za man.	مِنَ الزَّمنِ.
A minute is equal to	'aad da qîqa tö tö sã wî	اَلدَّقيقَةُ تُسَاوِى
sixty seconds,	sit tî na Ta ni ya tan	سِتِّينَ ثَانِيَةً
an hour is equal to	was sã a'a tö tö sã wî	وَالسَّاعَةُ تُسَاوِى
sixty minutes	sit tî na da qî qa tan	سِتِّينَ دَقِيقَةً
and a day	wal yaw mö	وَاليَومُ
is equal to	yö sã wî	يُسَاوِى
twenty four	'aarba a'an wa a'iŠ rîna	أَربَعاً وَ عِشرِينَ
hours.	sã a'a tan.	سَاعَةً.
My watch has	li sã a'a tî mî nã 'aön	لِسَاعَتِى
a bright dial	lã mi a'ön	مِيناءٌ لَامِعٌ
with figures.	ma a'al 'aar qãm.	مَعَ الأَرقَامِ.

123

English	Transliteration	Arabic
It has two hands:	ka mã la hã a'aq ra bãn:	كَمَالَهَا عَقْرَبَانِ :
One small hand	a'aq ra bön _S_a ghîr	عَقْرَبٌ صَغِيرٌ
and a big hand.	wa a'aq ra bön ka bîr.	وَعَقْرَبٌ كَبِيرٌ .
The small hand	al a'aq ra bö_S_ _S_a ghîr	اَلْعَقْرَبُ الصَّغِيرُ
points to hours	yö Šîr 'ai las sã a'ãt	يُشِيرُالىٰ السَّاعَاتِ
and the big hand	wal a'aq ra böl ka bîr	وَالْعَقْرَبُ الْكَبِيرُ
points to minutes.	yö Šîrö 'ai lad daqã'aiq.	يُشِيرُالىٰ الدَّقَائِقِ .
Every day	köl la yaw min	كُلَّ يَومٍ
in the morning	fi_S_ _S_ã bãH	فى الصَّبَاح
I leave	'aa_K_ rö jö	أَخْرُجُ
at 9.00, O'clock	fis sã a'a tit tã si a'a	فِى السَّاعَةِالتَّاسِعَةِ
for my school	li mad ra sa tî	لِمَدرسَتِى
and till 5.00	wa Hat tas sã a'a til	وَحَتىْ السَّاعَة
O'clock	_K_ã mi sa	الْخَامِسَة
I remain in the school.	'aab qã fil mad ra sa.	أَبْقىٰ فِى المَدْرَسَة .
At	fis sã a'a til	فِى السَّاعَةِ
5.30	_K_ã mi sa wan ni_S_ fi	الْخَامِسِةِوَ النّصف
I return to my home	'aa a'ð dö li man zi lî	أَعُودُ لِمَنزِلِى
and till	wa Hat tas sã a'a tis	وَحَتى السَّاعَة
7.00	sã bi a'a	السَّابِعَة

I play with	'aal a'a bö ma a'a	أَلْعَبُ مَعَ
my friends.	'aaS di qã 'aî.	أَصْدِقَائِى.
Then at	Tõm ma fis	ثُمَّ فِى
7.15	sã a'a tis sã bi a'a	السَّاعَةِ السَّابِعَةِ
	war rð ba'	وَالرُّبع
I sit down to revise	a'aj li söli mö rã ja a'ati	أَجْلِسُ لِمُرَاجِعَة
my lessons.	dö rð sî .	دُرُوسِى .
I revise my lessons	'aö rã ji a'ö dö rð sî	أَرَاجِعُ دُرُوسِى
till	Hat tas sã a'a tit	حَتىَّ السَّاعَة
8.45.	tã si a'a ti 'ail lãr röba'.	التَّاسِعَة الالرُّبع.
Then I eat	Tõm ma 'aã kö lö	ثُمَّ آكُلُ
my dinner	a'a Šã a'î	عَشَائى
at 9.00.	fis sã a'a tit tã si a'a.	فى السَّاعَةِ التَّاسِعَة.
After that till	baa' da Ðã lik Hat tas	بَعدَ ذَلِك حتى
10.00 O'clock	sã a'a til a'ã Ši ra'	السَّاعَةِ الْعَاشِرَة
we talk	na ta HaddaTö sawîyan	نَتَحَدَّثُ سَوِيا
and gossip. Then	wa nödar di Šö Tömma	وَنُدَرِدِش ثُمَّ
sleep comes to us.	yaa' tî nãn nawm.	يَأْتِينَا النَّومُ .
In the morning at	fiS Sa bãH fis	فى الصَّبَاح فى
6.00	sã a'a tis sã di sa	السَّاعَةِ السَّادِسَة

125

I wake up	'aa qð mö	أَقُومُ
from sleep	mi nan nawm	مِنَ النَّوم
and I go to	wa 'aaÐ ha bö 'ai lã	وَأَذهَبُ الى
the garden of our area	Ha dî qa ti Hã ra ti nã	حَدِيقَةِ حَارتِنَا
to revise my lessons.	limö rã ja a'a tid dörðs.	لِمُرَاجَعَةِ الدُّرُوس.
About 8.00	fis sã a'a tiT Tã mi na	فِى السَّاعَةِ الثَّامِنَةِ
O'clock	a'a lã waj hit taq rîb	علىٰ وَجهِ التَقرِيب
I return home	'aa a'ð dö lil man zil	أَعُودُ لِلمَنزِلِ
and take	wa a 'aã Kö Ðö	وَآخُذُ
bath and wear	Hammãmî wa 'aal basö	حَمَّامِى وَأَلبَسُ
clean clothes.	ma lã bis na zî fa.	مَلابِسَ نَظِيفَةً.
Then	Töm ma	ثُمَّ
I take my breakfast	'aã kö lö fö †ð rî	آكُلُ فُطُورِى
and take	wa 'aã 'Kö Ðö	وَآخُذُ
my tiffen carrier	a'ö mð da †a a'ã mî	عمُودَ طَعَامِى
for lunch	lil gha dã 'ai	لِلغَدَاءِ
and my satchel	wa Šan †a tî	وَشنطتى
and go to	wa 'aaÐ ha bö	وَأَذهَبُ
my school.	'ai lã mad ra sa tî.	الى مَدرَسَتِى.
In all this work	fî köllihã Ðihil 'aaa'mãl	فِى كُلِّ هَذه الاغمَالِ

126

English	Transliteration	Arabic
this watch helps me a lot.	tö sã a'i dö nî hã Ði his sã a'a tö ka *Tî* ran.	تُسَاعِدنِى هذه السَاعَةُ كَثِيرًا.

Exercise		التمرين
Question (1)		السؤال (١)
what is watch ?	mã hi yas sã a'a tö ?	مَاهِى السَّاعَة ؟
Answer		الجواب
The watch is an instrument	as sã a'a tö	اَلسَّاعَةُ
that points	'aã la tön ta döl lö	آلَةٌ تَدُلُّ
to time/tells time.	a'a laz za man.	عَلىٰ الزمن .
Question(2)		السؤال (٢)
Who gave you	man 'aaa' †ã ka	مَن أَعطَاك
your watch?	sã a'a tak?	سَاعَتَك؟
Answer		الجواب
My elder brother gave me	'aaa' †ã ni sã a'a tî	أَعطَانِى سَاعَتِى
my watch.	'aa <u>K</u>î 'aal ka bîr.	أَخِى الكَبِيرُ.
Question(3)		السؤال (٣)
Is your watch	hal sã a'a tök	هَلْ سَاعَتَك
beautiful?	ja mî la?	جَمِيْلَةٌ ؟

Answer		الجواب
Yes, my watch is	na a'am, sã a'a tî	نَعَمْ، سَاعَتِى
beautiful.	ja mî la.	جَمِيلَةٌ .
Question(4)		السؤال (٤)
Who taught	man a'al la mak	مَنْ عَلَّمَك
you to know time from	maa' ri fa taz za man	مَعْرِفَة الزَّمُنِ
the watch?	bis sã a'a?	بِالسَّاعَة ؟
Answer		الجواب
My brother taught me	a'al la ma nî 'aa <u>K</u>î	عَلَّمَنِى أَخِى
to know time	ma'a ri fa taz za man	مَعْرِفة الزَّمنِ
from the watch.	bis sã a'a.	بِالسَّاعَة .
Question(5)		السؤال (٥)
When do you leave	ma tã ta<u>K</u> rö jö	مَتىٰ تَخْرُجُ
for your school?	li mad ra sa tik?	لِمَدرَسَتِك ؟
Answer		الجواب
I leave for my school	'aa<u>K</u> röjö li mad rasa tî	أَخْرُجُ لِمَدرَسَتِى
at 9.00	fis sã a'a tit	فى السَّاعَةِ
O'clock	tã si a'a.	التَّاسِعَة.
Question(6)		السؤال (٦)
When do you return	ma tã ta a'ð dö	مَتىٰ تَعُودُ

English	Transliteration	Arabic
to your home?	li man zi lik?	لِمَنزِلِكَ ؟
Answer		الجواب
I return to my home	'aa a'ð dö li man zi lî	أَعُودُ لِمَنزِلِى
at 5.30.	fis sã a'a til	فِى السَّاعَةِ
	Ka mi sa wan niSf.	الخَامِسَةِ وَالنِّصف.
Question(7)		السؤال (٧)
When do you revise	ma tã tö rã ji a'ö	مَتىٰ تُرَاجِعُ
your lessons?	dö rð sak?	دُرُوسَك ؟
Answer		الجواب
I revise my lessons	'aö rã ji a'ö dö rð sî	أَرَاجِعُ دُرُوسِى
at	fis sã a'a tis	فِى
7.30.	sã bi a'a wan niSf.	السَّابِعَةِ وَالنِّصف.
Question(8)		السؤال (٨)
When do you sleep?	ma tã ta nãm?	مَتىٰ تَنَامُ ؟
Answer		الجواب
I sleep	'aa nãm	أَنَامُ
at 10.00	fis sã a'a til a'ã Ši ra	فِى السَّاعَةِ العَاشِرَة
O'clock.	a'a lã waj hit taq rîb.	عَلىٰ وَجهِ التَّقرِيب.
Question(9)		السؤال (٩)
When do you wake up	ma tã ta qöm	مَتىٰ تَقُومُ

from your sleep?	min naw mik ?	مِن نَومِك؟
Answer		الجَواب
I wake up	'aa qöm	أقُومُ
from my sleep	min naw mî	مِن نَومِى
at	fis sã a'a tis	فِى
6.00 O'clock'	sã di sa.	السَّاعَةِ السَّادِسَة.
Question(10)		السؤال(١٠)
Do you like	hal tö Hib bö	هَلُ تُحِبُّ
your watch?	sã a'a tak?	سَاعَتَك؟
Answer		الجَواب
Yes, I	na a'am ,'aa nã	نَعَمُ، أَنَا
like my watch.	'aö Hib bö sã a'a tî.	أُحُبُّ سَاعَتِى.

◄☆☆☆►

130

Lesson 19

Coversationمحادثة

Mr. Munir	as say yid mö nîr	اَلسَّيِّدُ منير
Ahmed	'aa*H* mad	أَحمَد
is an Iraqi national.	mö wã †in a'i rã qî.	مُوَاطِنٌ عِرَاقى.
He lives	hö wa yas kö nö	هُوَ يَسكُنُ
in Baghdad,	fî bagh dãd	فِى بغدَاد،
the capital of Iraq.	a'ã *S*i ma til a'i rãq.	عَاصِمَة العِرَاق.
He works there	wa yaa' ma lö hö nã ka	وَيَعمَلُ هناك
in a private office.	fî mak tab *KãS S*.	فِى مَكتَبٍ خَاصٌّ.
He is a big officer '	hö wa mö wa*z z*af kabîr.	هُوَ مُوَظَّفٌ كبيرٌ.
Mr. Munir	'as say yid mö nir	اَلسَّيِّد مُنير
Ahmed	'aa*H* mad	أحمد
loves touring	yo *H*ib bös si yã *Ha*	يُحِبُّ السِّيَاحَة
very much inside the	ka *Tî* ran fî	كثيرًا فى
country	dã *Ki* lil bî lãd	دَاخِلِ البِلَاد
and abroad.	wa *Kã* ri ji hi.	وَخَارِجِه.
Mr.	kã nas say yid	كَانَ السَّيِّد
Munir Ahmed	mö nîr 'aa*H* mad	منير أحمد
read about India	qa ra 'aa a'a nil hind	قَرَأ عَنِ الهند

131

and its historical	wa ma 'aā Ti ri hãt	وَمَآثِرها
monuments.	tā rî Kî ya.	التَارِيخيَّة.
It happend that he	fa Ha Sa la 'aan	فَحَصَلَ أَن
had opportunity,	ta waffa rat lahöl förSa	تَوَفَّرتُ لَه الفُرصَةُ
to visit New Delhi,	li zi yā ra ti ni yð dil hî,	لِزِيَارةِ نيودلهى،
India,	al hind,	الهِند،
a few months ago.	qab la Šö hðr.	قَبلَ شُهُورٍ.
Mr.	as say yid	السَّيِّد
Munir Ahmed	mö nir 'aaH mad	مُنيرأحمد
did not know	lam ya kön yaa' rif	لَم يَكُنْ يَعُرِفُ
anyone	'aa Ha dan	أَحَدًا
in New Delhi.	fî ni yð dil hî.	فى نيودلهى.
After clearance	fa baa' da Ka lā Si hi	فَبَعد خَلَاصِه
from customs	mi nal ja mā rik	مِنَ الجَمَارِك
Mr. Munir Ahmed left	Ka ra jas sayyid mönîr	خَرَجَ السَّيِّد مَنير
the arrival hall	min Sā la til wö Sðl	مِن صَالةِ الوُصول
to the taxi	'ai lā maw qi fis	الى مَوقِفِ
stand	say yā rāt	السَّيَّارَات
and took taxi.	wa 'aa Ka Ða tāk sî.	وَأَخَذَ تاكسى.
The taxi	fa sa 'aa la hö	فَسَألَه

132

English	Transliteration	Arabic
driver asked him:	sã 'ai qöt tãk sî:	سَائِقُ التاكسى:
Sir, where	say yi dî, 'aay na	سَيِّدى ،أين
do you want to go?	tö rî döÐ Ða hãb?	تُريدُ الذَهَابَ؟
Mr. Munir	as say yid mö nîr	السَّيِّد مُنير
Ahmed:	'aaHmad:	أحمد:
I want to go	'aö rî döÐ Ða hãb	أريدُ الذهَاب
to a hotel.	'ai lã fön döq.	الى فُندق.
I am new in	'aa nã ja dîd fî	أنَا جَديدٌ فى
this country.	hã Ðal ba lad.	هَذاالبَلَد.
Where is the	'aay na yð ja dö	أَيْنَ يُوجَدُ
best hotel?	'aaH san fön döq?	أحسن فندق؟
The taxi driver:	sã 'ai qöt tãk sî:	سَائِقُ التاكسى:
Let us go to	fal naÐ hab 'ai lã	فَلْنَذهَبْ الى
Ashok Hotel.	'aa Šðk hð tîl	أشوك هوتيل.
It is a five	hö wa fön döq	هُو فُندق
star hotel.	Kam sat nö jðm.	خَمسَة نُجُوم.
It is run by the	wa hö wal 'ai dã ra töl	وَهُو الاذارَةُ
government.	Hö kð mî ya.	الحُكوميَّة .
Mr. Munir	as say yid mönir	السَّيِّد مُنير
Ahmed:	'aaHmad :	أحمد:

English	Transliteration	Arabic
Where is it?	'aay na hö wa?	أينَ هُوَ؟
Is it far	hal hã Đã ba a'îd	هَل هَذا بَعيدٌ
from here ?	min hö nã?	مِن هنا؟
Taxi driver:	sã 'ai qöt tãk sî:	سَائِقُ التاكسى:
Yes' sir,	na a'am, yã say yi dî,	نَعَم، يا سيدى،
about half	ni_S_ fö sã a'a a'a lã	نِصفُ ساعةٍ على
an hour.	waj hit taq rîb.	وَجهِ التَقريب.
However, it is in	wa lã kin na hö fî	وَلكنَّه فى
the heart of the city	qal bil ma dî na	قَلبِ المَدينَة
and you can	wa yöm ki nö lak	وَيُمكِنُ لَك
move	at ta _H_ar rök	التَحَرُّك
easily.	bi sö hð la.	بِسهُولة.
Mr. Munir	as say yid mö nîr	اَلسَّيِّد مُنير
Ahmed	'aa_H_mad:	أحمد :
O.K. Let us go.	†ay yib, fal naĐ hab.	طَيِّب، فَلنَذهب.
Taxi driver:	sã 'ai qöt tãk sî:	سَائِقُ التاكسى:
Good, sir.	_H_ã _d_ir, yã say yi dî.	حَاضِر، ياسيدى.
Are you a tourist?	hal 'aan ta say yãh?	هَلُ أنتَ سَيَّاحٌ؟
Mr. Munir	as say yid mö nîr	اَلسَّيِّد مُنير
Ahmed:	'aa_H_mad:	أحُمَد:

English	Transliteration	Arabic
Yes' I am a tourist.	na a'am 'aanã sayyãH.	نَعَم، أَنَا سَيَّاح.
I heard and read	sa mia'tö wa qa ra'a tö	سَمِعتُ وَقَرَأْكُ
a lot about India	ka Tîran a'a nil hind	كَثِيرًا عَنِ الهند
and its historical	wa ma 'aã Ti ri hat	وَمَآثِرها
monuments.	tã rî Kî ya.	التَاريخية.
After a while	baa' da qa lîlin	بَعدَ قَليلٍ
the taxi reached	wa Sa lat tak sî	وَصَلَ التاكسى
Ashok Hotel.	'ai lã fön döq 'aa Šok.	الىٰ فُندُق أشوك.
Mr. Munir	ta ra ka as say yid mö	تَرَكَ السَّيِّد مُنير
Ahmed left the taxi,	nîr 'aaH mad at tãk sî	أحمد التاكسى
and entered the hotel.	wa da Ka lal fön döq.	وَدَخَلَ الفندق.
He went to	wa Đa ha ba 'ai la	وَذَهَبَ الى
the reception room.	ghör fa til 'ais tiq bãl.	غُرفَةِ الاسِتقبَال.
Reception	mö waz za föl	مُوَظَّفُ
officer	'ais tiq bãl	الاسِتقبَال
welcomes him!	yö raH Hib bi hi	يُرَحِّبُ به
They have the	wa yaj rî bay na hö mã	وَيَجرِى بَينَهُما
following conversation:	al Ha dî Tat tã lî:	الحَديثُ التَّالى.
Reception officer:	mö waz za föl'ais tiqbãl:	مُوَظَّفُ الاسِتقبَال:
Welcome!	'aah lan wa sah lan!	أهلًا و سَبُلًا!

135

Sir.	ʾyã say yi dî.	يَاسَيِّدى.
What can I do for you	'aay yö Kid ma?	أَىُّ خِدمَة؟
Mr. Munir	as say yid mönir	اَلسَّيِّد مُنير
Ahmed:	'aaHmad:	أحمد:
I want a room,	'aö rîd ghör fa tan	أَريدُ غُرفَةً
please.	min fadlik.	مِن فَضلِك.
Reception officer:	mö waz za föl 'ais tiq bãl:	مُوَظَّفُ الاسِتقبَال:
single bed	ghör fa tön ma a'a sa rîr	غُرفةٌ مَع سَريرٍ
or double bed?	'aaw ma a'a sarî rayn?	أو مَع سَريرَين؟
Mr. Munir	as say yid mö nîr	اَلسَّيِّد مُنير
Ahmed:	'aaHmad :	أحمد:
Single bed (room)	ghör fa ma a'a	غُرفة مَع
only.	sa rîr wã Hid.	سَريرٍوَاحد.
I want	'aö rîd	أَريدُ
a comfortable room	ghör fa mö rî Ha	غُرفَةً مُريحَة
with bathroom (attached).	ma a'al Ham mãm.	مَع الحَمَّام .
Reception officer:	mö waz za föl 'ais tiq bãl:	مُوَظَّفُ الاسِتقبَال:
We have	a'in da nã	عِندَنا
single bedroom	ghör fa sa rîr	غُرفَة سَرير
with bathroom.	ma a'al Ham mãm.	مَع الحَمَّام.

136

English	Transliteration	Arabic
It is hundred dollars per day.	sia' rö hã mi 'aat dö lãr lil yawm.	سِعرُهَا مِائة دُولار لِلُيَوم.
Mr. Munir Ahmed:	as say yid mö nir 'aaH mad :	اَلَسَّيِّد مُنير أحمد:
I want this room,	'aö rîd hã Đi hil ghör fa.	أَرِيدُ هذه الغُرفَة.
Reception officer:	mö waz za föl 'ais tiq bãl:	مُوَظَّفُ الاسِتِقبَال:
Your name?	mas mök?	مَا اسُمُك؟
Address?	wa a'ön wã nök?	وَ عُنوانُك؟
Purpose of your visit?	wa sa ba bözi yã ra tik?	وَ سَبَبُ زِيَارَتِك؟
Your nationality?	wa jin sî ya tök?	وَ جِنسِيَّتك؟
No. of	wa raqm	وَ رَقمُ
your passport?	ja wãz sa fa rik?	جَوازِ سَفرِك ؟
Mr. Munir Ahmed:	as say yid mö nîr 'aaH mad:	اَلَسَّيِّد مُنير أحمد:
My name is Munir Ahmed.	'ais mî mö nîr 'aaH mad.	اسمى مُنير أحمد.
I am from Iraq.	'aa nã mi nal a'i rãq.	أَنَا مِنَ العِرَاق.
I live in Baghdad,	'aas kö nö fî bagh dãd,	أسُكُنُ فى بغداد،
the capital of Iraq.	a'ã Si ma til a'i rãq.	عَاصِمةِ العِرَاق.
Purpose of my visit	sa bab zi yã ra tî	سَبَبُ زِيَارَتى

137

English	Transliteration	Arabic
is tourism.	'aas si yã Ha.	السِياحَة.
No. of my passport is	raqm ja wãzi sa fa rî	رَقم جَوَازسَفَرى
B/0123022,	B/0123022.	٠١٢٣٠٢٢/ب.
Reception officer:	mo waz za föl 'ais tiq bãl:	مُوَظَّفُ الاسِتِقبَال:
sir,	say yi dî,	سَيِّدى،
please,	min fad lik,	مِنْ فَضلِك،
for how many days	kam yaw man	كَم يَوماً
you'll stay here?	sa tö qî mö hö nã?	سَتُقِيمُ هنا؟
Mr. Munir	'aas say yid mö nîr	اَلسَّيِّد مُنير
Ahmed:	'aaHmad:	أحمد:
I don,t know/no idea.	lã 'aad rî.	لاأَدرى.
Perhaps for a week.	röb ba mã li 'aös böa'.	رُبَّمَا لأَسبُوع.
Reception officer:	mö waz za föl 'ais tiq bãl:	مُوَظَّفُ الاسِتِقبَال:
Your room No. is 15	raqm ghör fa tik 15	رَقمُ غُرفتك ١٥
on the first floor.	fid daw ril 'aaw wal.	فِى الدَّورِالاول.
Mr. Munir	as say yid mö nîr	اَلسَّيِّد مُنير
Ahmed thanks him	'aaHmad yaŠ kö rö hö	أحمد يَشكُرُه
and heads to	wa ya ta waj ja hö 'ai lã	وَيَتَوَجَّه الى
his room with	ghör fa ti hi ma a'a	غُرفَتِه مَعَ
a hotel worker/employee.	a'ã mi lil fön döq.	عَامِلِ الفندق.

English	Transliteration	Arabic
The worker opens	al a'ã mil yaf ta Hö	العَامِل يَفتَحُ
the room of Mr. Munir	ghör fa tas say yid	غُرفَةُ اَلسَّيِّد
Ahmed.	mö nîr 'aaH mad.	مُنير أحمد.
Mr. Munir	yad Kö lö as say yid	يَدخُلُ اَلسَّيِّد
Ahmed enters	mö nîr 'aaH mad	مُنير أحمد
his room.	ghör fa ta hö.	غُرفَتَه.
He finds it	wa ya ji dö hã	وَيَجِدُها
clean and	na zî fa tan wa	نَظِيفَةً وَ
comfortable.	mö rî Ha tan.	مُريحَةً.
It has all	fî hã köl lö	فِيهَا كُلُّ
facilities of comfort,	'aas bã bir rã Ha	أسبَابِ الرَاحَةِ
like	min 'aam Tã lis	مِنْ أمثَال
comfortable bed and	sa rîril mö rîH wal	السَريرالمُريح وَ
cosy chairs and	ka rã sî wal	الكَراسِى وَ
sofas,	ka na bã til wa Tî ra	الكَنبَات الوَثِيرَة
telephone	wat ti li fõn	وَالتلفون
and television.	wat ti li fız yõn.	وَالتلفزيون.
Mr.	ya qð lös say yid	يَقُولُ اَلسَّيِّد
Munir Ahmed says	mö nir 'aaH mad	مُنير أحمد
to the worker:	lil a'ã mil:	لِلعَامِل:

139

English	Transliteration	Arabic
Now I want	al 'aã na 'aö rîd	الآنَ أُريدُ
to rest	al 'ais ti rã Ha	الاستِراحَة
and I don,t want	wa lã 'aö rîd	وَ لا أُريدُ
any thing else.	Šay 'aan 'aã Ka ra.	شَيئاً آخَر.
The woker understands	al a'ã mi lö	العَامِل يَفهَم
the meaning.	yaf ha möl ma† lðb.	المَطلُوب.
He leaves the baggage	wa yat rö köl a'a faŠ	وَ يَترُكُ العَفَش
beside the bed	bi jã ni bis sa rîr	بِجَانِبِ السَّرير
and leaves.	wa yaK rö jö.	وَ يَخرُج.
Mr. Munir	as say yid mö nîr	اَلسَّيِّد مُنير
Ahmed	'aaH amd	أحمد
closes the room	yögh li qöl ghör fa	يُغلِقُ الغُرفَةَ
and goes to the	wa yaÐ ha bö	وَيَذهَبُ الى
bed to sleep.	'ai las sa rîr li ya nãm.	السَرِيرِ لِيَنَام.

Exercise

التمرين

Question (1)

السؤال (١)

Who is Mr.		مَن هُوَاَلسَّيِّد
Munir Ahmed?	man hö was say yid	مُنير أحمد؟
	mö nîr 'aaH mad?	

English	Transliteration	Arabic
Answer		الجواب
Mr. Munir	as say yid mö nîr	اَلسَّيِّد مُنير
Ahmed	'aaH mad	أحمد
is an Iraqi national.	mo wã †i nön a'i rã qî.	مُوَاطِنٌ عِرَاقى.
Question (2)		السؤال(٢)
Why did Mr. Munir	limã Đã jã 'aa 'aas say	لِمَاذَا جَاءَ السَّيِّد
Ahmed come	yid mö nîr 'aaH mad 'ai	مُنير أحمد
to New Delhi ?	lã ni yð dil hî?	الى نيودلهى ؟
Answer		الجواب
Mr. Munir Ahmed	as say yid mö nîr	اَلسَّيِّد مُنير
is a tourist.	'aaH mad say yã Hön.	أحمد سَيَّاح.
He came to New Delhi	jã 'aa 'ai lã ni yð dil hî	جَاءَ الى نيودلهى
to visit historical	li zi yã ra til ma 'aã Tir	لِزِيَارَة المَآثِر
monuments.	'aat tã rî Kî ya.	التَارِيخِيَّة.
Question (3)		السؤال(٣)
What does Mr. Munir	mã Đã ya qð lös say	مَاذَايَقُولُ السَّيِّد
Ahmed say	yid mö nîr 'aaH mad	مُنير أحمد
to the taxi driver?	li sã 'ai qit tãk sî?	لِسَائِق التاكسى ؟
Answer		الجواب
Mr.	ya qð lös say yid	يَقُولُ السَّيِّد

141

English	Transliteration	Arabic
Munir Ahmed says	mö nîr 'aaH mad	مُنير أحمد
to the taxi driver:	li sã 'ai qit tãk sî:	لِسَائق التاكسى:
I want to go	'aö ri döÐ Ða hãb	أُريدُ الذَّهَابَ
to some hotel.	'ai lã fön döq.	الى فُنْدُق.
Question (4)		السؤال (٤)
Where does the taxi driver	'aay na yaÐ ha bö bi hi	أينَ يَذهَبُ به
go with him/take him?	sã 'ai qöt tãk sî?	سَائقُ التاكسى؟
Answer		الجواب
The taxi driver	yaÐ ha bö bi hi	يَذهَبُ به
takes him	sã 'ai qöt tãk sî	سَائق التاكسى
to Hotel Ashok	'ai la fön döq 'aa Šðk	الى فُندُق أشوك
run by	at tã bia'	التَابِع
the government	lil Hö kð ma til	لِلْحُكُومَةِ
of India.	hin dî ya.	الهِندِيَّةِ.
Question (5)		السؤال (٥)
Where is	'aay na yð ja dö	أينَ يُوجَدُ
this hotel?	hã Ðal fön döq?	هَذاالفندق؟
Answer		الجواب
This hotel is	yð ja dö hã Ðal fön döq	يُوجَدُ هَذَاالفُندق
in the heart of the city	fî qal bil ma dî nã	فى قَلبِ المَدِينَة

from where	min *Hay Tö*	مِنْ حَيثُ
movement	yöm ki nöt ta *H*ar rök	يُمكِنُ التَحَرُّك
is easy.	bi sö hð la.	بِسُهولَة.
Question (6)		السؤال(٦)
Is Mr. Munir	ha lis say yid mö nîr	هَل السَّيِّد مُنير
Ahmed	'aa*H* mad	أحمد
a tourist?	say yã *H*ön?	سَيَّاح ؟
Answer		الجواب
Yes. Mr.	na a'am, 'aas say yid	نَعَمْ، اَلسَّيِّد
Munir Ahmed	mö nîr 'aa*H* mad	مُنير أحمد
is a tourist.	say yã *H*ön.	سَيَّاح.
Question (7)		السؤال(٧)
Where is he from?	min 'aay na hö wa?	مِنْ أينَ هُو؟
Answer		الجواب
He is from Baghdad,	hö wa min bagh dãd,	هُو مِنْ بَغْدَاد،
the capital of Iraq.	a'ã <u>S</u>i ma til a'i rãq.	عَاصِمَةِ العِرَاق.
Question (8)		السؤال(٨)
What does	mã Ðã	مَاذَا
Mr. Munir Ahmed	yaf a'a lö as say yid	يَفعَل اَلسَّيِّد
do	mö nîr 'aa*H* mad	مُنير أحمد

143

English	Transliteration	Arabic
after he arrives	baa' da wö _Sð_ li hi	بَعدَ وُصُوله
at the hotel ?	'ai lãl fön döq?	الى الفندق؟
Answer		الجواب
After he reaches	baa' da wö _Sð_ li hi	بَعدَ وُصُوله
the hotel,	'ai lal fön döq	الى الفُندق
Mr.	ya† lö bös say yid	يَطلُبُ اَلسَّيِّد
Munir Ahmed asks for	mö nîr 'aa_H_ mad	مُنير أحمد
a single	ghör fa tan Ðã ta	غُرفَةً
bedroom	sa rî rin wã _H_id	ذَاتَ سَرير وَاجد
with bathroom (attached)	ma a'al _H_am mãm.	مَعَ الحَمَّام .
Question (9)		السؤال (٩)
How does Mr.	kay fa ya ji dös say yid	كَيفَ يَجِدُ السَّيِّد
Munir Ahmed find	mö nîr 'aa_H_ mad	مُنير أحمد
this room?	hã Ði hil ghör fa?	هَذه الغُرفَة ؟
Answer		الجواب
Mr. Munir Ahmed finds	ya ji dös say yid	يَجِدُ اَلسَّيِّد
	mö nîr 'aa_H_ mad	مُنير أحمد
this room	hã Ði hil ghör fa	هَذه الغُرفَة
clean and	na _zî_ fa tan wa	نَظيفَةً وَ
comforable	mö rî _H_a tan	مُريحَةً

144

with all neccessary	ma a'a köl lil 'aaŠ yã	مَعَ كُلًّ الاشيَاء
things	'aid da rð rî ya	الضَرُورِيَّة
like	min 'aam Tã lit	مِنْ أمثال
television and	ti li fiz yðn	التلفزيون و
telephone	wat ti li fðn	التلفون
etc.	wa mã 'ai lã Ðã lik.	و ما الى ذلك.
Question (10)		السؤال(١٠)
What does Mr.	mã Ðã ya qð lös say yid	مَاذا يَقُولُ اَلسَّيِّد
Munir Ahmed say	mö nir 'aaH mad	مُنير أحمد
to the worker	li a'ã mi lil	لِعَامِلٍ
of the hotel?	fön döq?	الفُندق؟
Answer		الجواب
Mr.	ya qð lös say yid	يَقُولُ السَّيِّد
Munir Ahmed says	mö nir 'aaH mad	مُنير أحمد
to the worker of the hotel:	li a'ã mi lil fön döq:	لِعَامِلِ الفندق:
I want	'aö rî döl 'aã nal	أريدُ
to take rest now.	'ais ti rã Ha ta.	الآنَ الاسِتِرَاحَة.
Question (11)		السؤال(١١)
What does the	mã Ðã yaf a'a lö	مَاذاَ يَفعَل
hotel worker do?	a'ã mi löl fön döq?	عَامِل الفُنْدق؟

145

Answer		الجواب
The hotel worker	a'ã mi löl fön döq	عَامِل الفُنْدق
understands	yaf ha möl	يَفْهَمُ
the meaning	ma† löb	المَطلُوب
and he leaves	wa yat rö köl	وَيَترُك
the baggage	a'a faŠ	العَفَش
and leaves	wa yaK röj	وَ يَخرُجُ
the room.	mi nal ghör fa.	مِنَ الغُرفَة.
Question(12)		السؤال(١٢)
What does	mã Đã yaf a'a lös	مَاذَا يَفعَل
Mr. Munir	say yid mö nîr	اَلسَّيِّد مُنير
Ahmed do?	'aaH mad?	أحمد؟
Answer		الجواب
Mr. Munir	as say yid mö nîr	اَلسَّيِّد مُنير
Ahmad	'aaH mad	أحمد؟
closes the door	yögh li qöl bãb	يُغلِقُ البَابَ
and he goes	wa yaĐ ha bö	وَ يَذهَبُ
to the bed	'ai las sa rîr	الى السَرِير
to sleep.	li ya nãm.	لِيَنَامَ.

❖☆☆☆❖

146

Lesson 20

حكاية من حكايات شاشا شكن
One of the Tales of Uncle Chakkan

There was a man who	kã na ra jö lön	كَان رَجُلٌ
lived in	yas kö nö fî	يَسكُنُ فى
India	bi lã dil hi nd	بِلادِ الهِند
once upon	fî za ma nin mi nal	فى زَمَنٍ مِن
a time.	'aaz mãn.	الأزْمَانِ.
There was	wa mã kã na	وَ مَاكَانَ
none	'aa Ha dön	أَحَدٌ
who knew his	yad rîs ma hö	يَذرِى إِسمَه
real name,	al Ha qî qî	الحَقِيقى
but all the	wa lã kin na ja mî a'an	ولٰكِنَّ جَمِيعَ
people	nã si kã nð	النّاسِ كَانُوا
called him	yad a'ð na hö bis mi "Šã	يَدعُونَه باسم
"Chacha Chakkan".	Šã Šak kan".	"شاشا شكن".
The word chacha	wal ka li ma tö 'Šã Šã'	وَالكَلِمةُ 'شاشا'
is a Hindi word	ka li ma tön hin dî ya tön	كَلِمَةٌ هِندِيّةٌ
which means 'Uncle'.	taa' nî "al a'amm".	تَعنى "العم".
This way Chakkan	hã ka Ðã kã na Šakkan	هٰكَذَا كَانَ شكن

147

English	Transliteration	Arabic
was everybody's uncle.	a'am man lil ja mîa'.	عمّاً لِلْجَميع.
Uncle Chakkan	kã nal a'amm Šak kan	كَانَ العَمُّ شكن
was very miserly	ba Kî lan jid dan	بَخيلًا جِدًّا
and egoist /	wa 'aa nã nî yan	وَ أَنَانِيًا
self centred .	lil ghã ya.	لِلْغَايَة.
A good number of	yör wã a'a dad ka bîr	يُرْوَى عَدَدٌ كَبيرٌ
stories are told	mi nal Hî kã ya ti a'an	مِنَ الحِكَايَاتِ عَنْ
about his miserliness and	böK li hî wa	بُخْلِهِ وَ
ego.	'aa nã nî ya ti hi	أَنَانِيَّتِهِ.
I'll tell you	'aaÐ kö rö la köm	أَذْكُرُ لَكُمْ
one such story	Hi kã ya tan	حِكَايَةً
that would speak of his	ta döl lö a'a lã	تَدُلُّ عَلى
miserlines	böK li hi	بُخْلِهِ
and ego.	wa 'aa nã nî ya ti hi.	وَ أَنَانِيَّتِه.
Title of	a'ön wãn	عُنْوَانُ
this story is	hã Ði híl Hi kã ya	هَذه الحِكَاية
Chacha Chakkan	Šã Šã Šak kan	شاشاشكن
and his donkey.	wa Hî mã rö hö.	وَ حِمَارُه.
Once a friend	mar ra tan 'aa tã	مَرَّةً أتى
came	Sa dî qön	صَديقٌ

148

English	Transliteration	Arabic
to uncle Chakkan	'ai lã Šã Šã Šak kan	الى شاشاشكن
and said:	wa qã la:	وَقَالَ:
Uncle Chakkan,	yã a'amm Šak kan	ياَ عَمُّ شكن،
I want	'aö rî d	أُريدُ
to travel to the neighboring	'an 'aö sã fi ra 'ai lãl qar	أَن أُسَافِرَ الى
village for	ya til mö jã wi ra	القَرْيَةِ المُجَاوَرَةِ
an urgent piece of work,	fî a'a ma lin a'ãjil,	فى عَمَلٍ عَاجِلٍ،
but I don't have a mount	wa lã kin mã a'in dî	وَلٰكِنْ مَاعِندى
/riding animal,	ma ïî ya,	مَطِيَّة،
Lend me,	'aa a'ir nî	أعِرْنى
please,	min fad lik	مِنْ فَضْلِك
your donkey.	Hi mã rak.	جِمَارَك.
He added saying:	wa 'aa dã fa qã 'ai lan:	وَ أضَافَ قَائِلاً:
I'll return to you your	sa 'aör ji a'ö lak	سَأُرجِعُ لَك
donkey	Hi mã rak	جِمَارَك
in the evening	fil ma sã 'ai	فى المَسَاءِ
and pay	wa 'aad fa a'ö lak	وَ أدفعُ لَك
rental for that.	'aöj ra tan a'a lay hi.	أجرَةً عَليه.
Uncle Chakkan replied	rad dal a'am mö	رَدَّ العَمُّ
saying:	Šak kan qã 'ai lan:	شكن قَائِلا:

149

I am	'ain na nî	اننى
very sorry	'aã sif jid dan	آسِفٌ جِدّاً
my friend	yã Sa dî qî.	يَا صَدِيقى.
I can not answer	lã 'aas ta †î a'ö	لَا أسْتَطِيعُ
your request	'aan 'aö jî ba †a la bak	ان أُجِيبَ طَلَبَك
because the donkey	li 'aan nal Hi mã ra	لانَّ الجِمَارَ
is not here.	lay sa hö nã.	لَيسَ هُنا.
Hardly	wa lam yö tim ma	وَلَمْ يُتِمّ
Uncle Chakkan had	al a'am mö Šak kan	العَمُّ شكن
finished that	ka lã ma ho Hat tã	كَلَامَه حَتى
the donkey began to	ba da 'aa al Hi mã rö	بَدَأ الجِمَارُ
bray in	yan ha qö fi	يَنهَقُ
his enclosure.	Ha zî ra ti hi.	فى حَظِيرته.
His friend heard	sa mi a'a Sa dî qö hö	سَمِعَ صَدِيقُه
the donkey's bray	na hî qal Hi mãr	نَهِيق الجِمَارِ
and he found the matter	was tagh ra bal	وَ استَغرَبَ
strange.	'aam ra.	الامْرَ.
He said to him :	wa qã la la hö:	وَ قَالَ لَهَ:
I hear your donkey	'ain na nî 'aas ma a'ö	اننى أسْمَعُ
bray O' Uncle	Hi mã rak yã a'am mö	جِمارَك يَاعَمُّ

English	Transliteration	Arabic
Chakkan.	Šak kan yan haq.	شكن يَنهَقْ.
Uncle was angry	fa gha *d*i bal a'am mö	فَغَضِبَ العَمُّ
and replied saying:	wa rad da qã 'ai lan:	وَ رَدَّ قَائِلاً:
your matter is strange	gha rî bön 'aam rök	غَرِيبٌ أَمْرُك
my friend.	yã _S_a dî qî.	يَا صَدِيقى.
Are you going to believe	'aa tö _S_ad di qöl	أَ تُصَدِّقُ
the donkey	*H*i mãr	الجِمَارَ
and belie me?	wa tö kaĐ Đi bö nî?	وَتُكَذِّ بُنى؟

Exercise | التمرين

Question (1)		السؤال(١)
Who is Chacha	man hö wa Šã Šã	مَنْ هو شاشا
Chakkan?	Šak kan?	شكن؟
Answer		الجواب
Chacah Chakkan was an	kã na Šã Šã Šak kan	كَانَ شاشا شكن
Indian man	ra jö lan hin dî yan	رَجُلاً هِنْدِيًّا
in the ancient times.	fî ghã bi ril 'aaz mãn.	فى غَابِرِ الازْمَانِ.
Question(2)		السؤال(٢)
How was	kay fa kã na	كَيفَ كَانَ
Chacha Chakkan?	Šã Šã Šak kan?	شاشا شكن؟

151

Answer		الجواب
Chacha Chakkan was	kã na Šã Šã Šak kan	كَانَ شاشاشكن
very miserly	ba Kîlan jid dan	بَخِيلًا جِدًّا
and	wa 'aa nã nî yan	وَ أَنَانِيّاً
egoistic.	lil ghã ya ti.	لِلغَايَةِ.
Question(3)		السؤال (٣)
What is the title of the	mã a'ön wã nol	مَا عُنوانُ
story	Hi kã ya til	الحِكَايَةِ
you read about	la tî qa ra'a ta ha a'an	التى قَرَأَتَها عَنْ
Chacha Chakkan?	Šã Šã Šak kan?	شاشا شكن؟
Answer		الجواب
The title of this	a'ön wãn hã Đi hil Hi	عُنوانُ هَذه
story	kã ya ti	الحِكَايَةِ
is Chacha Chakkan and	"Šã Šã Šak kan wa	"شاشا شكن و
his donkey	Hi mã rö hö".	حِمَاره".
Question(4)		السؤال(٤)
Who came	man qa di ma 'ai la	مَنْ قَدِم الى
to Chacha Chakkan?	Šã Šã Šak kan?	شاشا شكن؟
Answer		الجواب
Once his friend came	mar ra tan qa di ma	مَرَّةً قَدِمَ

English	Transliteration	Arabic
to Chacha Chakkan.	'ai la Šã Šã Šak kan Sa dî qö hö.	الى شاشا شكن صَديقُه.
Question(5)		السؤال(٥)
What did his friend ask Chacah Chakkan?	mã Đã qã la Sa di qö hö li Šã Šã Šak kan?	مَاذَا قَالَ صَديقُه لشاشا شكن؟
Answer		الجواب
His friend asked him	†a la ba min hö	طَلَبَ منه
(for) his donkey	Sa dî qö hö Himã ra hö	صَديقُه جِمَاره
because	li 'aan na hö	لِانَّه
he wanted to go	0'aa rã daĐ Đa hã ba	أرَادَ الذّهَاب
to the	'ai lal qar ya til	الى القَريَة
neighbouring village.	mö jã wi ra.	المُجَاورَة.
Question(6)		السؤال (٦)
How did Chacha Chakkan reply?	kay fa 'aa jã ba Šã Šã Šak kan?	كَيفَ أَجَابَ شاشا شكن؟
Answer		الجواب
Chacha Chakkan	'aa jã ba hö	أَجَابَه
replied	Šã Šã Šak kan	شاشاشكن
that the donkey	'aan nal Himã ra	أنَّ الجِمَازَ
was not in (there).	lay sa hö nã.	لَيسَ هنا.

153

Question(7)		السؤال(٧)
What did happen	mã Ðã Ha Sa la	مَا ذَا حَصَلَ
at that time?	fî Ðã li kal waqt?	فى ذَلِكَ الوَقتِ؟
Answer		الجواب
At the same time	fî naf sil waq ti	فى نَفسٍ الوَقت
the donkey began	ba da 'aal Hi mã rö	بَدَأ الحِمَارُ
to bray.	yan ha qö.	يَنهَقُ.
Question(8)		السؤال(٨)
What did the friend say	mã Ðã qã laS Sa dî qö	مَاذَا قَالَ الصَّدِيقُ
to Chacha Chakkan?	li Šã Šã Šak kan?	لشاشا شكن؟
Answer		الجواب
It is a strange thing	hã Ðã Šay 'aön a'a jîb	هَذاشىءٌ عَجِيبٌ
Uncle Chakkan.	yã a'amm Šak kan.	يَاعَمُّ شكن.
I hear	'ain na ni 'aas ma a'ö	اننى أسمَعُ
your donkey bray.	Hi mã rak yan haq.	حِمَارَك يَنهَق.
Question(9)		السؤال (٩)
How did Uncle Chakkan	kay fa 'aa jã ba hö	كَيفَ أجَابَه
reply?	al a'amm Šak kan?	العَمُّ شكن؟
Answer		الجواب
Uncle Chakkan became	gha di bal a'amm	غَضِبَ العَمُّ

154

English	Transliteration	Arabic
angry	Šak kan	شَكِن
and said:	wa qã la:	وَقَالَ:
your matter is strange my	gha rî bön 'aam rök	غَرِيبٌ أمرُك
friend!	yã Sa dî qî!	يَا صَدِيقى!
Do you believe the	'aa tö Sad di qöl	أتُصَدِّقُ
donkey	Hi mã ra	الجِمَارَ
and belie me ?	wa tö kaĐ Đi bö nî?	وَ تَكذِّبُنى ؟
Question(10)		السؤال(١٠)
How do you find	kay fa ta ji dö	كَيفَ تَجِدُ
this soty?	ha Đi hil Hi kã ya?	هَذِه الحِكَايَةَ؟
Answer		الجواب
This story is	ha Đi hil Hi kã ya tö	هَذه الحِكَايةُ
very interesting.	mom ti a'a tön jid dan.	مُمْتِعَةٌ جِدًّا.
Question(11)		السؤال(١١)
Do you remember	hal taĐ kö rö Hi kã ya	هَل تَذكُرُ جِكَايَة
a similar story ?	tan mö mã Ti la tan?	مُمَاثِلَةً؟
Tell	'öĐ kör	أذكُرُ
a similar	hi kã ya tan	جِكَايَة
story	mö mã Ti la tan	مُمَاثِلَةً
briefly.	bi 'aî jãz.	بِايجَازٍ.

◈☆☆☆◈

Glossary

'aa lif   الف

Miss (of girl)	'aã ni sa	آنسة
father	'aab	أب
alphabetical	'aab ja dî	ابجدى
alphabet	al *H*ö r*ð*f al 'aab ja dîya	الحروف الابجدية
I change	'aö bad di lö	ابدل
I remain	'aab qã	ابقى
son	'aibn	ابن
wayfarer	'aib nös sa bîl	ابن السبيل
doors	'aab wãb	ابواب
white	'aab ya*d*	ابيض
He came	'aa tã	أتى
furniture	'aa *T*ã*T*	أثاث
two	'ai*T* nã ni	اثنان
clothes	'aa*T* wãb	اثواب
leave/vacation	'ai jã za	اجازة
I find	'aa ji dö	اجد
hire/rental/wage	'aöj ra	اجرة
I sit	'aaj li sö	اجلس

156

foreigner	'aaj na bî	اجنبى
I answer	'aö jîb	اجيب
I love/like	'aö *H*ibb	احب
I need	'aa*H* tãj	احتاج
anyone	'aa *H*a dan	احدا
better	'aa*H* san	احسن
sometimes	'aa*H* yã nan	احيانا
brother	'aa<u>K</u>	أخ
inform	'aa<u>K</u> bir (imp.)	اخبر
inform e us	'aa<u>K</u> bir nã (imp.)	اخبرنا
sister	'aök tön	اخت
I take	'aã <u>K</u>ö Ðö	آخذ
he took	'aa <u>K</u>a Ða	أخذ
I took	'aa <u>K</u>aÐ tö	أخذت
another	'aã <u>K</u>a rö	آخر
I leave	'aa<u>K</u> rö jö	اخرج
other	'aö<u>K</u> rã	اخرى
brothers	'aik wa tön	اخوة
last	'aa <u>K</u>îr	اخير
administration	'ai dã rã /al 'ai dã rã	ادارة /الادارة

manners	'aa dab	ادب
I study /read	'aad rö sö	ادرس
I know	'aad rî	ادرى
I pay	'aad fa a'ö	ادفع
floors	'aad wãr	ادوار
I go	'aaÐ ha bö	اذهب
I return	'aar ji a'ö	ارجع
I revise	'aö rã ji a'ö	اراجع
twenty four	'aar ba a'an wa a'iŠ rîna	اربعا وعشرين
forty	'aar ba a'ðn	اربعون
I request you	'aar jŏk	ارجوك
sincerity	'ai<u>K</u> lã<u>S</u>	اخلاص
rice	'aö röz/al 'aö röz	ارز/الارز
floor	'aar *d*î ya	ارضية
figures	'aar qãm	ارقام
villages	'aar yãf	ارياف
I want	'aö rîd	اريد
blue	'aaz raq	ازرق
sky blue	'aaz raq sa mã wî	ازرق سماوى
times	'aaz mãn	ازمان

158

I am sorry	'aã sif	آسف
I travel	'aö sã fir	اسافر
reasons	'aas bãb	اسباب
week	'aös bða'	اسبوع
two weeks	'aös bð a'ayn	اسبوعين
teacher/professor	'aös taÐ	استاذ
rest	'ais ti rã Ha	استراحة
I can	'aas ta †î a'ö	استطيع
he found strange	'ais tagh ra ba	استغرب
reception	'ais tiq bãl	استقبال
drawing room	ghör fa töl 'ais tiq bãl	(غرفة الاستقبال)
I live	'aas kö nö	اسكن
name	'aism	اسم
names	'aas mã 'aö	اسماء
your name	'ais mök	اسمك
my name	'ais mî	اسمى
black	'aas wad	اسود
questions	'aas 'ai la	اسئلة
trees	'aaŠ jãr	اشجار
things	'aaŠ yã'a	اشياء

finger	'ai<u>S</u> baa'	اصبع
friends	'aa<u>S</u> di qã 'aö	اصدقاء
younger/smaller	'aa<u>S</u> ghar	اصغر
he added	'aa *d*ã fa	اضاف
doctors	'aa †ib bã 'aö	اطباء
foods	'aa† a'i ma	اطمعة
lend/give	'aa a'ir (imp.)	اعر
lend me	'aa a'ir nî(imp.)	اعرنى
he gave you	'aaa' †ãk	اعطاك
he gave him	'aaa' †ã hö	اعطاه
work/jobs	'aaa' mãl	اعمال
their work	'aaa' mã lö höm	اعمالهم
I return	'aa a'ð dö	اعود
closing	'aigh lãq	اغلاق
most of the times	'aagh la böl 'aa*H* yãn	اغلب الاحيان
at most of the times	(fî'aagh la bil 'aa*H* yãn)	(فى اغلب الاحيان)
open(s. m.)	'aif ta*H*(imp.)	افتح
open (s. f.)	'aif ta *H*î(imp.)	افتحى
open (p. f.)	'aif ta*H*na (imp.)	افتحن
open (p. m.)	'aif ta *H*ð(imp.)	افتحوا

160

better	'aaf *da* lö	افضل
I (will) do	'aaf a'a lö	افعل
pictures	'aaf lãm	افلام
I (will) meet	'aö qã bi lö	اقابل
stay	'ai qã ma	اقامة
my stay	'ai qã ma tî	اقامتى
feet	'aaq dãm	اقدام
relatives	'aaq ri bã'a	اقرباء
locks	'aaq fãl	اقفال
pens	'aaq lãm	اقلام
I get up	'aa qð mö	اقوم
I (will) stay	'aö qî mö	اقيم
I (will) eat	'aã kö lö	آكل
write (s. f.)	'aök tö bî(imp.)	اكتبى
more	'aak *Ta* rö	اكثر
now	al 'aã na	الآن
I (will) wear	'aal ba sö	البس
who (s. m.)	al la Ðî	الذى
I (will) play	'aal a'a bö	العب
thousand	'aalf	الف

Allahabad	al lãh 'aã bãd	الله اباد
Germany	al mã ni yã	المانيا
to	'ai lã	الى
see you/bye	'ai lal li qã'a	الى اللقاء
machine	'aã lã	آلة
mother	'aömm	ام
examination	'aim ti *H*ãn	امتحان
like	'aam *T*ãl	امثال
like	(min 'aam *T*ãl)	(من امثال)
order	'aam rön	امر
woman	'aim ra 'aa tön	امراة
your order	'aam rök	امرَك
American	'aam rî kî	امريكى
I (will) walk	'aam Šî	امشى
fill	'aim la'a (imp.)	املأ
or	'aam	ام
as regard	'aam mã	اما
that	'ain na ('aan na)	ان
I	'aa nã	أنا
I (will) sleep	'aa nãm	انام

162

egoist	'aa nã nî	انانى
egotism	'aa nã nî ya	انانية
you (s. m.)	'aan ta	انت
you (s. f.)	'aan ti	انت
wait	'ain ti z̲ãr	انتظار
in your wait	(fin ti z̲ã rik)	(فى انتظارك)
regularity	'ain ti z̲ãm	انتظام
you two (m. f.)	'aan tö mã	انتما
you (p. f.)	'aan tön na	انتن
it ended	'ain ta hã	انتهى
completing	'ain jãz	انجاز
If God so wills	'ain Šã 'aal lãh	ان شاء الله
nose	'aanf /'aan fön	انف
leopards	'aan mãr	انمار
rivers	'aan hãr	انها ر
welcome	'aah lan wa sahlan	اهلاوسهلا
	biköm	بكم
autobus/bus	'að tð bîs	اوتوبيس
buses	'að tð bî sãt	اوتوبيسات
valleys	'aaw di ya	اودية

163

papers	'aaw rãq	اوراق
times	'aaw qãt	اوقات
first	'aaw wal	اول
boys	'aaw lãd	اولاد
those (m. f.)	'að lã 'aik	اولئك
ice cream	'aays ki rîm	ايس كريم
also	'aay dan	ايضا
days	'aay yãm	ايام

(ب)

door	bãb	باب
cold	bã rid	بارد
stinginess	böK̲l	بخل
stingy	ba K̲îl	بخيل
he began	ba da 'aa	بدأ
full moon	badr	بدر
without	bi ðn	بدون
cooler	bar rãd	برّاد
cold	bard	برد
mail/post	ba rîd	بريد

164

post office	(mak ta böl ba rîd)	(مكتب البريد)
gardener	bös tã nî	بستانى
duck	ba††	بط
card	bi †ã qa	بطاقة
arrival card	(bi †ã qa töl wö sðl)	(بطاقة الوصول)
belly, stomach	ba†an	بطن
after	baa'd	بعد
some	baa' dö nã	بعضنا
far/distant	ba a'îd	بعيد
Baghdad	bagh dãd	بغداد
remander	ba qî ya	بقية
country	bi lãd	بلاد
country	ba lad	بلد
girls	ba nãt	بنات
two girls	bin tãn	بنتان
bank	bank	بنك
ice cream	bð za	بوظة
house	bayt	بيت
eggs	bayd	بيض
between	bay na	بين

165

between them	bay na hö mã	بينهما
houses	bö yðt	بيوت
		(ت)
trader/ business	tã jir	تاجر
you take	ta'a <u>K</u>öÐ	تأخذ
historical	tã rî <u>K</u>î (s. m. adj.)	تاريخى
historical	tã rî <u>K</u>î ya (s. f. adj.)	تاريخية
nineth	tã si a'a	تاسعة
nine O'clock	(as sã a'a at tã si a'a)	(الساعة التاسعة)
visa	ta'a Šî ra	تأشيره
taxi	tãk sî	تاكسى
following	tã lî	تالى
those two (d. f.)	tã ni ka	تانك
exchange/change	tab dîl	تبديل
commercial	ti jã rî ya	تجارية
you (will) find	ta ji dö	تجد
you (will) find us	ta ji dö nã	تجدنا
renewal	taj dîd	تجديد
you love /like	tö *H*ib bö	تحب

166

movement	ta *H*ar rök	تحرك
greeting	ta *H*î ya	تحية
it indicates	ta döl lö	تدل
you remember	ta*Ð* kö rö	تذكر
you (will) go / she (will) go	ta*Ð* ha bö	تذهب
you (will) revise	tö rã ji a'ö	تراجع
you (will) guide	tör Ši dö	ترشد
you (will) guide me	tör Ši dö nî	ترشدنى
he left	ta ra ka	ترك
you want	tö rîd	تريد
you (will) help me	tö sã a'i dö nî	تساعدنى
it is equal	tö sã wî	تساوى
you live	tas kö nö	تسكن
tired	taa' bãn	تعبان
you know / she knows	taa' rif	تعرف
eduaction	taa' lîm	تعليم
it means	taa' nî	تعنى
incubation	taf rî<u>K</u>	تفريخ
please	ta fa*d d*al	تفضل
about / around	taq rî ban	تقريبا

167

you say/she says	ta qð lö	تقول
you get up/she gets up	ta qð mö	تقوم
you stay /she stays	tö qîm	تقيم
you write/she writes	tak tö bö	تكتب
you believe me	tö kaÐ Ði bö nî	تكذبنى
pupils/students	ta lã mîÐ	تلاميذ
you wrap/she wraps	ta löf fö	تلف
television	ti li fiz yðn	تلفزيون
telephone	ti li fðn	تلفون
that (fem.)	til ka	تلك
pupil/student	til mîÐ	تلميذ
extension	tam dîd	تمديد
you walk/she walks	tam Šî	تمشى
you sleep /she sleeps	ta nãm	تنام
he headed towards	ta waj ja ha	توجه
it was available	ta waf fa ra (m.)	توفر
it was available	ta waf fa rat (mas.)	توفرت

(ث)

eight	*Ta* mi na	ثامنة
second	*Ta* ni ya	ثانية

thirty	Tal lã Tõ na	ثلاثون
refrigerators	Tal lã jat	ثلاجات
refrigerator	Tal lã ja	ثلاجة
then	Tõm ma	ثم
eighty	Ta mã nõn	ثمانون
fruit	Ta mar	ثمر
price	Ta man	ثمن
expensive	Ta mîn	ثمين
clothe	Tawb	ثوب

(ج)

he came	jã 'aa	جاء
universities	jã mi a'ãt	جامعات
side	jã nib	جانب
beside	(bi jã nib)	(بجانب)
ready	jã hiz	جاهز
cheese	jöb na	جبنة
forehead	jab ha	جبهة
forehead	ja bîn	جبين
grandfather	jadd	جد

169

very much	jid dan	جدا
new	ja dî da	جديدة
grandmother	jad da	جدة
bell	ja ras	جرس
he ran	ja ra	جرى
part/portion	jöz ön	جزء
customs	ja mã rik	جمارك
beauty	ja mãl	جمال
camels	ji mãl	جمال
custom (of duty)	jöm rök	جمرك
all	ja mîa'	جميع
beautiful	ja mîl	جميل
beautiful	ja mî la	جميلة
soldier	jön dî	جندى
natoinality	jin sî ya	جنسية
army, soldiers	jö nðd	جنود
pound	jö nayh	جنيه
answer	ja wãb	جواب
passport	ja wãz	جواز
your passport	ja wãz sa fa rik	جوازسفرك

hungry	jaw a'ãn	جوعان
I came	ji'a tö	جئت
generation	jîl	جيل

(ح)

eyebrow	Hã jib	حاجب
need	Hã ja	حاجة
locality	Hã ra	حارة
our locality	Hã ra tö nã	حارتنا
present	Hã dir	حاضر
condition/state	Hãl	حال
wall	Hã 'ai†	حائط
till	Hat tã	حتى
gardens	Ha dã 'aiq	حدائق
fix	Had did	حدد
conversation	Ha dîT	حديث
garden	Ha dî qa	حديقة
belt	Hi zãm	حزام
it (so) happened	Ha Sal	حصل
we attended	Ha dar nã	حضرنا

171

English	Transliteration	Arabic
enclosure	*H*a z̲î ra	حظيرة
pit	*H*öf ra	حفرة
real	*H*a qî qî	حقيقى
stories	*H*i kã yãt	حكايات
story	*H*i kã ya	حكاية
governmental	*H*ö kð mî ya	حكومية
milk	*H*a lîb	حليب
donkey	*H*i mãr	حمار
bath	*H*am mãm	حمام
bathroom	*H*a mãm	حمام
my bath	*H*am mã mî	حمامى
paise	*H*amd	حمد
all praise be to God	(al *H*am dö lil lãh)	(الحمدلله)
tap	*H*a na fî ya	حنفية
as / whereas	min *H*ay *T*ö	(من حيث)

(خ)

English	Transliteration	Arabic
servant	K̲ã dim	خادم
outside	K̲ãrij	خارج
special / private	K̲ã*SS*	خاص

172

special/private	K̲ã̲S̲ S̲a tön	خاصة
uncle (maternal)	K̲ãl	خال
empty/free	K̲ã lî	خالى
aunty (maternal)	K̲ã la	خالة
fifth	K̲ã mi sa	خامسة
5 O'clock	(as sã a'a al K̲ã mi sã)	(الساعة الخامسة)
bread	K̲öbz	خبز
take	K̲öÐ (imp.)	خذ
servant	K̲a dam	خدم
he left/went out	K̲a ra ja	خرج
we left	K̲a raj nã	خرجنا
trunk	K̲ör tðm	خرطوم
going out	K̲ö rðj	خروج
waist	K̲iS̲r	خصر
vegetables	K̲öd rã wãt	خضروات
watchman	K̲a fîr	خفير
rescue/acquittal	K̲a lãS̲	خلاص
five	K̲ams	خمس
five	K̲am sa	خمسة
fifteen	K̲am sa ta a'a Ša ra	خمسة عشر

173

twenty five	<u>K</u>am sa tön wa a'iŠ rðn	خمسة وعشرون
thinking	<u>K</u>a yãl	خيال
image	<u>K</u>a yãl	خيال
nostril	<u>K</u>ay Šðm	خيشوم

(د)

always	dã 'ai mãn	دائما
chicken	da jãj	دجاج
inside	dã <u>K</u>il	داخل
he entered	da <u>K</u>a la	دخل
bi-cycles	dar rã jãt	دراجات
bi-cycle	dar rã ja	دراجة
studies	di rã sãt	دراسات
study	di rã sã	دراسة
lesson	dars	درس
lessons	dö rðs	دروس
minutes	da qã 'aiq	دقائق
minute	da qî qa	دقيقة
shop	dök kãn	دكان
cupboards	da wã lîb	دواليب

174

inkpot	da wãt	دواة
floor	dawr	دور
first floor	(ad dawr al 'aaw wal)	(الدور الاول)
cinema halls	dõ röl Kay ãl	دورالخيال
toilet	daw ra töl mi yãh	دورة المياه
cupboard	dõ lãb	دولاب
dollar	dõ lãr	دولار
dollars	dõ lã rãt	دولارات

(ذ)

having/consisting of	Đã ta	ذات
those two (d. m.)	Đã ni ka	ذانك
chin	Điqn	ذقن
mention	Đikr	ذكر
that (s. m.)	Đã li ka	ذلك
going	Đa hãb	ذهاب
wolves	Đi 'aãb	ذئاب
wolfs	Đi'a bön	ذئب

(ر)

comfort	rã Ha	راحة
head	ra'a sön	رأس

1/4 one fourth	röb a'ön	ربع
perhaps	röb ba mã	ربما
men	ri jãl	رجال
man	ra jöl	رجل
leg	rijl	رجل
cheap	ra Kis	رخيص
answer/reply	radd	رد
painter	ras sãm	رسام
painters	ras sã mǒn	رسامون
official	ras mî	رسمى
official (fem.)	ras mî ya	رسمية
freinds/companions	rö fa qã'a	رفقاء
friend / companion	ra fîq	رفيق
figure	raqm	رقم
knee	rök ba	ركبة
it rang	ran na	رن
rupees	rðb yãt	روبيات
rupee	rðb ya	روبية
heads	rö 'aðs	رووس
heads/chiefs	rö 'aa sã	رؤوساء

176

kind/compassionate	ra 'aðf	رؤوف
head/president	ra 'aîs	رئيس
village	rîf	ريف
		(ز)
visitor	zã 'air	زائر
butter	zöb da	زبدة
customer/client	za bŏn	زبون
crop	zara'	زرع
time	za man	زمن
colleague	za mîl	زميل
visitors	zŏw wãr	زوار
husband	zawj	زوج
wife	zaw ja	زوجة
visits	zi yã rãt	زيارات
visit	zi yã ra	زيارة
		(س)
seventh	sã bi a'a	سابعة
7 O'clock	(as sã a'a as sã bi a'a)	(الساعة السابعة)
sixth	sã di sa	سادسة

177

English	Transliteration	Arabic
6 O'clock	(as sã a'a as sã di sa)	(الساعة السادسة)
arm	sã a'id	ساعد
watch	sã a'a	ساعة
he travelled	sã fa ra	سافر
shank	sãq	ساق
I will stay	sa 'aö qîm	ساقيم
resident	sã kin	ساكن
he asked	sa 'aa la	سأل
driver	sã 'aiq	سائق
drivers	sã 'ai qðn	سائقون
reason	sa bab	سبب
seven	sab a'a	سبعة
blackboards	sab bð rãt	سبورات
blackboard	sab bð ra	سبورة
you will stay	sa tö qîm	ستقيم
sixty	sit tîn	ستين
carpet/mat	saj jã da	سجادة
happiness	sö rðr	سرور
bed	sa rîr	سرير
two beds	sa rî rayn	سريرين

178

navel	sör ra	سرة
rate	sia'r	سعر
its rate	sia' rö hö	سعره
journey	sa far	سفر
knives	sa kã kîn	سكاكين
residents	sök kãn	سكان
residence	sa kan	سكن
silence	sö kðn	سكون
knife	sik kîn	سكين
peace	sa lã ma	سلامة
he heard	sa mi a'a	سمع
she heard	sa mi a'at	سمعت
fish	sa mak	سمك
age	sinn	سن
centimeter	san tî mî tar	سنتيميتر
sandwiches	san wî Šãt	سندويشات
year	sa na	سنة
facility	sö hð la	سهولة
easily	(bi sö hð la)	(بسهولة)
boundary wall	sör	سور

179

English	Transliteration	Arabic
will/shall	saw fa	سوف
together	sa wî yan	سويا
tourist	say yãH	سياح
tourism	si yã Ha	سياحة
motorcars	say yã rãt	سيارات
motorcar	say yã ra	سيارة
my dear sir	say yi dî	سيدى
Mr	as say yid	السيد
he'll stay	sa yö qîm	سيقيم
bad	say yi 'aa	سيئة

(ش)

English	Transliteration	Arabic
road	Šã ria'	شارع
thankful	Šã kir	شاكر
tea	Šã 'ay	شاى
windows	Ša bã bîk	شبابيك
window	Šöb bãk	شباك
tree	Ša ja ra	شجرة
purchase	Ši rã'a	شراء
conditon	Šar†	شرط

company	Ša ri ka	شركة
conditons	Šö rð†	شروط
tape/cassette	Ša rî†	شريط
hair	Šaa'r	شعر
lip	Ša fa	شفة
full brother	Ša qîq	شقيق
full sister	Ša qî qa	شقيقة
thanks	Šök ran	شكرا
thanks a lot	Šök ran ja zîlan	شكراجزيلا
satchel/bag	Šan †a	شنطة
months	Šö hðr	شهور
famous	Ša hîr	شهير
roads	Ša wã ria'	شوارع
soup	Šðr ba	شوربة
thing	Šay	شىء

(ص)

shopkeeper	_S_ã _H_i böl ma _H_al li	صاحب المحل
hall	_S_ã la	صالة
arrival hall	_S_ã la al wö sðl	صالة الوصول

181

maker/manufacturer	_S_ã nia'	صانع
morning	_S_a bã_H_	صباح
good morning	_S_a bã _H_al _K_ayr	صباح الخير
good morning	_S_a bã _H_an nðr	صباح النور
in the morning	_S_a bã _H_an	صباحا
chest	_S_adr	صدر
friend	_S_a dîq	صديق
banker/money changer	_S_ar rãf	صراف
bankers	_S_ar rã fðn	صرافون
difficult	_S_aa'b	صعب
difficult	_S_aa' ba (fem.)	صعبة
small/younger	_S_a ghîr	صغير
class/row	_S_aff	صف
purity/clealiness	_S_a fã'a	صفاء
designation	_S_ifa	صفة
eagle	_S_aqr	صقر
eagles	_S_ö qðr	صقور
boxes	_S_a nã dîq	صناديق
box	_S_ön dðq	صندوق
water tank	_S_ih rîj	صهريج

woolen	_S_ð fî/ _S_ð fî ya	صوفى/صوفية
summer	_S_ayf	صيف

(ض)

captain/officer	_d_ã bi†	ضابط
captains/officers	_d_öb bã†	ضباط
udder	_d_ira'	ضرع
necessary	_d_a rð rî/_d_a rð rî ya	ضرورى/ضرورية

(ط)

was fine	†ã ba	طاب
good day	†ã ba yaw mök	طاب يومك
student	†ã lib	طالب
girl students	†ã li bãt	طالبات
girl student	†ã li ba	طالبة
tables	†ã wi lãt	طاولات
table	†ã wi la	طاولة
peacock	†ã 'að s	طاؤوس
aircrafts	†ã 'ai rãt	طائرات
aircraft	†ã 'ai ra	طائرة
cook	†ab bã_K_	طباخ

183

chalk	†a bã Šîr	طباشير
curry	†a bîḴ	طبيخ
dish/plate	†a baq	طبق
food	†a a'ãm	طعام
baby/child	†ifl	طفل
two babies/children	†if lãn	طفلان
students	†öl lãb	طلاب
demand	†a lab	طلب
tomato	†a mã †im	طماطم
peacocks	†a wã wîs	طواويس
pilot	†ay yãr	طيار
pilots	†ay yã rðn	طيارون
fine, O.K.	†ay yib	طيب

(ظ)

unjust	ẕã lim	ظالم
unjusts (pl.)	ẕã li mðn	ظالمون
nail	ẕöfr	ظفر
injustice/wrong	ẕölm	ظلم
phenomena	ẕa wã hir	ظواهر

184

back	ẕahr	ظهر
noon	ẕöhr	ظهر
		(ع)
worshipper	a'ã bid	عابد
urgent	a'ã jil	عاجل
ordinarily	a'ã da tan	عادة
unmarried	a'ã zib	عازب
tenth	a'ã Ši ra	عاشرة
10 O'clock	(as sã a'a al a'ã Ši ra)	(الساعة العاشرة)
capital	a'ã Ṣi ma	عاصمة
general/public	a'ã mm	عام
worker	a'ã mil	عامل
workers	a'ã mi lðn	عاملون
general/public	a'ãm ma	عامة
family	a'ã 'ai lî ya (adj.)	عائلية
servants of God	a'i bãd	عباد
servant of God	a'abd	عبد
strange /queer	a'a jîb	عجيب
number	a'a dad	عدد

185

a few	a'id da	عدة
Iraqi	a'i rã qî	عراقى
Arabic	a'a ra bî	عربى
dinner	a'a Šã'a	عشاء
ten	a'a Ša ra	عشر
twenty	a'iŠ rðn	عشرون
juice	a'a S̲îr	عصير
thirsty	a'at Šãn	عطشان
bones	a'i z̲am	عظام
luggage	a'a faŠ	عفش
he taught	a'al la ma	علم
he taught me	a'al la ma nî	علمنى
pardon me	a'af wan	عفوا
hand (of watch)	a'aq rab	عقرب
hands (two)	a'aq ra bãn	عقربان
on	a'a lã	على
approximately	a'a lã waj hit taq rîb	على وجه التقريب
uncle	a'amm	عم
work	a'a mal	عمل
workers	a'öm mãl	عمال

currencies	a'öm lãt	عملات
work/operation	a'a ma lî ya	عملية
currency	a'öm la	عملة
age	aömr	عمر
your age	a'öm rök	عمرك
my age	a'öm rî	عمرى
tiffin box	a'ö mŏd	عمود
aunty (paternal)	a'am ma	عمة
about	a'an	عن
at/with	a'in da	عند
with you / you have	a'in dak	عندك
when	a'in da mã	عندما
with me / I have	a'in dî	عندى
neck	a'ö nöq	عنق
address	a'ön wãn	عنوان
bread	a'ayŠ	عيش

(غ)

past	ghã bir	غابر
garcon/waiter	ghãr sŏn	غارسون

maximum/much	ghã ya	غاية
too much	lil ghã ya	(للغاية)
dust	ghö bãr	غبار
embezzlement	gha ban	غبن
tomorrow	gha dan	غدا
lunch	gha dã'a	غداء
strange	gha rîb	غريب
rooms	ghö rö fãt	غرفات
room	ghör fa	غرفة
anger	gha *d*ab	غضب

(ف)

bill	fã tõ ra	فاتورة
Varanasi	fã rã na sî	فاراناسى
persian	fã ri sî	فارسى
thigh	fa K̲iĐ	فخذ
chick/chicken	fi rãK̲	فراخ
pleasure, happiness	fa ra*H*	فرح
peon	far rãŠ	فراش
floor	farŠ	فرش

188

English	Transliteration	Arabic
opportunity	för _S_a	فرصة
French	fö ran sî (mas.)	فرنسى
Fernch	fö ran sî ya (fem.)	فرنسية
class / class room	fa_S_l	فصل
your class	fa_S_ lök	فصلك
my class	fa_S_ lî	فصلى
please	fa_d_ lik / min	فضلك / من
	fa_d_ lik	فضلك
breakfast	fö †ðr	فطور
thought	fik ra	فكرة
mouth	fam	فم
hotel	fön döq	فندق
in	fî	فى
elephant	fîl	فيل
in it	fî hã	فيها

(ق)

English	Transliteration	Arabic
able	qã bil	قابل
able	qã bi la (fem.)	قابلة
coming	qã dim	قادم

judge	qã *dî*	قاضى
hall	qã a'a	قاعة
he said	qã la	قال
she said	qã lat	قالت
Cairo	qã hi ra /al qã hi ra	قاهرة /القاهرة
saying	qã 'ai lan	قائلا
list/menu	qã 'ai ma	قائمة
before	qab la	قبل
he came	qa di ma	قدم
she came	qa di mat	قدمت
he read	qa ra 'aa	قرأ
she read	qa ra 'aat	قرأت
villages	qö ran	قرى
village	qar ya	قرية
near/close	qa rîb	قريب
palace	qa*S*r	قصر
palaces	qö *S*ör	قصور
judges	qö *d*ãt	قضاة
train	qi †ãr	قطار
cats	qi †a†	قطط

190

bite/he bit	qa *da* ma	قضم
heart	qalb	قلب
pen	qa lam	قلم
lock	qöfl	قفل
say	qöl	قل
tell us	qöl la nã	قل لنا
little	qa lîl	قليل
after some time	(baa' da qa lîl)	(بعد قليل)
shirts	qöm Şãn	قمصان
shirt	qa mîŞ	قميص
coffee	qah wã	قهوة

		(ك)
clerk	kã tib	كاتب
infidel	kã fir	كافر
he was	kã na	كان
big	ka bîr	كبير
big	ka bî ra (fem.)	كبيرة
book	ki tãb	كتاب
two books	ki tã bãn	كتابان

191

your book	ki tã bök	كتابك
books	kö töb	كتب
he wrote	ka ta ba	كتب
shoulder	ka tif	كتف
much	ka Tîr	كثير
very much	ka Tî ran	كثيرا
like that	ka Ðã lik	كذلك
notebook	kör rã sãt	كراسات
two notebooks	kör rã sa tãn	كراستان
chairs	ka rã sî	كراسى
chair	kör sî	كرسى
copy	kör rã sa	كراسة
ankle	kaa'b	كعب
palm	kaff	كف
infidels	köf fãr	كفار
dogs	ki lãb	كلاب
dog	kalb	كلب
words	ka li mãt	كلمات
word	ka li ma	كلمة
all	köl lö	كل

colleges	köl lî yãt	كليات
college	köl lî ya	كلية
how much	kam	كم
as/like	ka mã	كما
sweeper	kan nãs	كناس
sofa	ka na bãt	كنبات
purse	kîs	كيس
how	kayf	كيف
how are you?	kay fal Hãl	كيف الحال

(ل)

for	li	ل
no	lã	لا
don't write	lã tak töb (s. m.)	لاتكتب
don't write	lã tak tö bî (s. f.)	لاتكتبى
don't write	lã tak tö bð (p. m.)	لاتكتبوا
bright	lã mia'	لامع
able	lã 'aiq	لائق
meat	laHm	لحم
with	la dã	لدى

193

English	Transliteration	Arabic
with us /we have	la day nã	لدينا
delicious	la ÐîÐ	لذيذ
tongue	li sãn	لسان
languages	lö ghãt	لغات
language	lö gha	لغة
French language	al lö gha al fö ran sî ya	(اللغة الفرنسية)
wrap	löf fa (imp.)	لف
wrap it	löf fa hö (imp.)	لفه
meeting	li qã'a	لقاء
but	lã kin	لكن
but	wa lã kin	(ولكن)
was not	lam /lam ya kön	لم / لم يكن
he did not know	lam ya kön yaa' rif	لم يكن يعرف
why	li mã Ðã	لماذا
colour	lawn	لون
ability	li yã qa	لياقة
not	lay sa	ليس
night	layl	ليل

194

no, not	mã	ما
monuments	ma 'aã *Tir*	مآثر
what	mã Đã	ماذا
water	mã'a	ماء
hundred	mi 'aa	مائة
hunderd and fify	mi 'aa wa <u>K</u>am sŏn	مائة و خمسون
directly	mö bã Ša ra tan	مباشرة
married	mö ta zaw wij	متزوج
spectators	mö ta far ri jîn	متفرجين
when	ma tã	متى
neighbouring	mö jã wi ra	مجاورة
conversation	mö *H*ã da *T*a	محادثة
respected	mö*H* ta ram	محترم
fixed	mö *H*ad dad (mas.)	محدد
fixed	mö *H*ad dŏ da (fem.)	محددة
only/purely	ma*H* *d*a	محضة
shop	ma *H*all	محل
Mohammad	mö *H*am mad	محمد

195

sentrypost	ma<u>K</u> far	مخفر
schools	ma dã ris	مدارس
teacher	mö dar ris	مدرس
two teachers	mö dar ri sãn	مدرسان
school	mad ra sa	مدرسة
lady teacher	mö dar ri sa	مدرسة
lady teachers	mö dar ri sãt	مدرسات
two lady teachers	mö dar ri sa tãn	مدرستان
teachers	mö dar ri sõn	مدرسون
director	mö dîr	مدير
city	ma dî na	مدينة
radio	miÐ yaa'	مذياع
announcer	mö Ðia'	مذيع
announcers	mö Ðî a'ðn	مذيعون
revision	mö rã ja a'a	مراجعة
fans	ma rã wi*H*	مراوح
lavatory	mir *H*ãd	مرحاض
pencil/brush	mir sam	مرسم
central	mar ka zî	مركزى
once	mar ra tan	مرة

196

fan	mir wa Ha	مروحة
comfortable	mö rîH (mas.)	مريح
comfortalbe	mö rî Ha (fem.)	مريحة
evening (in the)	ma sã 'aan	مساء
distance	ma sã fa	مسافة
registrar	mö saj jil	مسجل
boiled	mas lðq	مسلوق
project	maŠ rða'	مشروع
busy	maŠ ghðl	مشغول
egypt	miSr	مصر
egyptian	miS rî	مصرى
airport	ma †ãr	مطار
obeyed	mö †ãa'	مطاع
restaurant	ma† a'am	مطعم
needed	ma† lðb	مطلوب
mount	ma †î ya	مطية
umbrellas	mi zal lãt	مظلات
umbrella	mi zal la	مظلة
wronged	maz lðm	مظلوم
wronged (plural)	maz lð mðn	مظلومون

197

with	ma a'a	مع
with peace	ma a'as sa lã ma	مع السلامة
place of worship	ma a'ã bid	معابد
meanings	ma a'ã nî	معانى
place of worship	maa' bad	معبد
counted	maa' dðd	معدود
wrist	mia' Sam	معصم
teacher/instructor	mö a'al lim	معلم
with him	ma a'a hö	معه
keys	ma fã tiH	مفاتيح
key	miftãH	مفتاح
minced	maf rðm	مفروم
size	ma qãs	مقاس
office	ma kã tib	مكاتب
letters	ma kã tîb	مكاتيب
place	ma kãn	مكان
office	mak tab	مكتب
letter	mak tðb	مكتوب
library	mak ta ba	مكتبة
meeting	mö qã ba lã	مقابلة

accepted	maq bðl	مقبول
fried	maq lî	مقلى
staying/resident	mö qîm	مقيم
clothes	ma lã bis	ملابس
full	ma lî 'aa	مليئة
similar	mö mã Til	مماثل
interesting	mö m tia'	ممتع
representative	mö maT Til	ممثل
rubber/eraser	mim Hãt	ممحاة
possible	möm kin	ممكن
who	man	من
from	min	من
delegate	man dðb	مندوب
delegates	man dð bðn	مندوبون
house	man zil	منزل
sought after	man Šðd	منشود
that you wanted	man Šð dak	منشودك
place of alighting	mah bi†	مهبط
expedition/misson	mö him ma	مهمة
official mission/work	mö him ma ras mî ya	مهمة رسمية

199

profession	mih na	مهنة
engineer	mö han dis	مهندس
agreed	mö wã fiq	موافق
present	maw jõd	موجود
official/employee	mö waz zaf	موظف
officials/employees	mö waz za fõn	موظفون
appointment	maw a'id	موعد
our appointment	maw a'i dö nã	موعدنا
stand	maw qif	موقف
bus stand	maw qi fõs say yã rãt	موقف السيارات
ground	may dãn	ميدان
dial	mi nã'a	ميناء

(ن)

we (will) take	na'a KöÐ	نأخذ
people	nãs /an nãs	ناس (الناس)
headmaster	nã zir	ناظر
plants	na bã tãt	نباتات
we (will) talk	na ta Had daT	نتحدث
success	na jãH	نجاح

200

my success	na jã *H*i	نجاحى
we find	na ji dö	نجد
stars	nö jŏm	نجوم
we (will) come	na jî 'aö	نجى ء
we	na*H* nö (m. f.)	نحن
we gossip	nö dar diŠ	ندردش
we (will)go	naĐ hab	نذهب
let us go	fal naĐ hab	(فلنذهب)
picnics	nöz hãt	نزهات
women	ni sã'a	نساء
half	ni_S_f	نصف
lot/ luck	na _Sî_b	نصيب
clean	na z̲î̲f/ na z̲î̲ fa	نظيف ⁄ نظيفة
yes	na a'am	نعم
we (will) work	naa' mal	نعمل
same	nafs	نفس
at the same time	(fî naf sil waqt)	(فى نفس الوقت)
we will be	na kð nö	نكون
we will meet	nal ta qî	نلتقى
leopard	na mir	نمر

201

number	nim ra	نمرة
kind	nawa'	نوع
day time	na hãr	نهار
end	ni hã ya	نهاية
river	nahr	نهر
bray	na hîq	نهيق
sleep	nawm	نوم
New Delhi	ni yð dil hî	نيودلهى

(ﻫ)

alighting	hã bi†	هابط
bring	hãt (imp.)	هات
these two	hã tã ni (fem.)	هاتان
telephone	hã tif	هاتف
take	hãk (imp.)	هاك
he alighted	ha ba †a	هبط
this	hã Ðã (mas.)	هذا
these two	hã Ðã ni (mas.)	هذان
these two	hã Ðay ni (mas.)	هذين
in this way	hã ka Ðã	هكذا

this	hã Ði hî	هذه
interrogative e.g. Is? am ?does ?etc	hal	هل
they (men)	höm	هـم
they two	hö mã (mas. fem.)	هما
here	hö nã	هنا
Indian	hin dî	هندى
India	al hind	الهند
they (women)	hön na	هن
he	hö wa	هو
telephones	ha wã tif	هواتف
these	hã 'að lã 'ai (m. f.)	هؤلاء
she	hi ya	هى

(و)

one	wã hid	واحد
valley	wã ðî	وادى
father	wã lid	والد
mother	wã li da	والدة
luxurious	wa *Ti* ra	وثيرة

203

faces	wö jðh	وجوه
face	wajh	وجه
rosy	war dî	وردى
paper	wa raq	ورق
minister	wa zîr	وزير
he arrived	wa S̲a la	وصل
arrival	wö S̲ðl	وصول
job	wa z̲î fa	وظيفة
time	waqt	وقت
boy	wa lad	ولد
two boys	wa la dã ni	ولدان

(ى)

he comes to us	ya'a tî na	يأتينا
he takes	ya'a K̲ö Ðö	يأخذ
they (two men) take	ya'a K̲ö Ðã ni	يأخذان
he changes	yö bad di lö	يبدل
he speaks	ya ta Had da Tö	يتحدث
he leaves	yat rök	يترك
he finishes	yö tim mö	يتم

204

he did not finish	lam yö tim ma	(لم يتم)
he heads	ya ta waj ja hö	يتوجه
it is neccessory	ya ji bö	يجب
he finds	ya ji dö	يجد
he finds (it/her)	ya ji dö hã	يجدها
he renews it	yö jad di dö hã	يجددها
he runs	yaj rî	يجرى
they (two men) go out	ya<u>K</u> rö jãn	يخرجان
hand	ya dön	يد
he enters	yad <u>K</u>öl	يدخل
he teaches	yad rös	يدرس
he knows	yad rî	يدرى
they invite	yad a'ð na	يدعون
they invite him	yad a'ð na hö	يدعونه
he welcomes	yö ra*H* *H*i bö	يرحب
he replies.	ya röd dö	يردّ
he responds		
he narrates	yar wî	يروى
left(side)	ya sãr	يسار
he travels	yö sã fi rö	يسافر

205

he asks	yas 'aa lö	يسأل
it equals	yö sã wî	يساوى
he lives	yas kö nö	يسكن
he hands over	yö sal li mö	يسلم
he listens	yas ma a'ö	يسمع
he buys	yaŠ ta rî	يشترى
he thanks	yaŠ kö rö	يشكر
he thanks him	yaŠ kö rö hö	يشكره
he indicates	yö shi rö	يشير
he puts	ya *d*a a'ö	يضع
he puts it	ya *d*a a'ö hã	يضعها
he asks, he demands	ya† lö bö	يطلب
it will be objected to	yöa' ta ra *d*ö a'a lay hi	يعترض عليه
he counts	ya a'öd dö	يعد
he counts it	ya a'öd dö hã	يعدها
he knows	yaa' ri fö	يعرف
he works	yaa' ma lö	يعمل
they work	yaa' ma lõ na	يعملون
he closes	yöq li qö	يغلق
he opens	yaf ta *H*ö	يفتح

206

he inspects	yö fat ti Šö	يفتش
he inspects him	yö fat ti Šö hö	يفتشه
he does	yaf a'a lö	يفعل
he understands	yaf ha mö	يفهم
he says	ya qð lö	يقول
he stays	yö qi mö	يقيم
they write	yak tö bð na	يكتبون
it consists of	ya ta kaw wan min	يتكون من
he completes	yök mi lö	يكمل
he will be	ya kð nö	يكون
they (will) complete	yök mi lð na	يكملون
he puts on	yal ba sö	يلبس
will be possible	yöm ki nö	يمكن
he fills	yam la 'aö	يملأ
right (side)	ya mîn	يمين
he calls	yö nã dî	ينادى
he calls him	yö nã dîhi	يناديه
he sleeps	ya nã mö	ينام
he looks	yan z̲ö rö	ينظر
it brays	yan ha qö	ينهق

it is found	yð ja dö	يوجد
it will reach	yð _Si_ lö	يوصل
it will reach you	yð _Si_ lök	بوصلك
day	yawm	يوم
your day	yaw mök	يومك
two days	yow mayn	يومين
monday	yaw möl 'ai _T_ nayn	يوم الاثنين
sunday	yam möl 'aa _H_ ad	يوم الاحد
tuesday	yaw mö _T Tö_ lã _Tã_ 'a	يوم الثلاثاء
friday	yaw möl jöm a'a	يوم الجمعة
thursday	yaw möl _Ka_ mîs	يوم الخميس
saturday	yaw mös sabt	يوم السبت

❈☆☆☆❈